THE ETHIC
HACKIN

Ross W. Bellaby

BRISTOL
UNIVERSITY
PRESS

First published in Great Britain in 2023 by

Bristol University Press
University of Bristol
1–9 Old Park Hill
Bristol
BS2 8BB
UK
t: +44 (0)117 374 6645
e: bup-info@bristol.ac.uk

Details of international sales and distribution partners are available at bristoluniversitypress.co.uk

© Bristol University Press 2023

British Library Cataloguing in Publication Data
A catalogue record for this book is available from the British Library

ISBN 978-1-5292-3181-6 hardcover
ISBN 978-1-5292-3182-3 paperback
ISBN 978-1-5292-3183-0 ePub
ISBN 978-1-5292-3184-7 ePdf

The right of Ross W. Bellaby to be identified as author of this work has been asserted by him in accordance with the Copyright, Designs and Patents Act 1988.

Cover design: Hayes Design and Advertising
Front cover image: Getty/Fotograzia
Bristol University Press use environmentally responsible print partners
Printed and bound in Great Britain by CPI Group (UK) Ltd, Croydon, CR0 4YY

FSC
www.fsc.org
MIX
Paper | Supporting
responsible forestry
FSC® C013604

For Matthew

Contents

Introduction

Over the last two decades, political hackers, like the infamous Anonymous collective, have demonstrated their digital power and a willingness to use that power for their own political agenda. As communications, data, finances, activities, businesses and personal information become increasingly digitized and realized through the Internet, the birth of the modern information nation means that states and individuals are significantly dependent on cyberspace to survive, something that has not escaped the attention of the hacking community. Indeed, hackers have proven that they can exert significant power over individuals, corporations and even states, illustrating their technical ability and desire to influence the world through cyber-attacks. During this time they have shut down government websites across the globe; hacked Amazon, PayPal and Mastercard, costing $5.5 million in damages; aided in the Arab Spring revolutions by enabling secure communication between revolutionaries; released private corporate information; and attacked media companies over anti-piracy. And most recently, they have declared war on the Russian Federation following the invasion of Ukraine, releasing military information and hijacking state-owned media (Chirinos, 2022; Tidy, 2022). However, in a world increasingly obsessed with superheroes and villains, what do hackers represent?

On the one hand, political hackers have been criticized and automatically denounced for acting outside the state apparatus, taking the law into their own hands (Thomas, 2002; Serracino-Inglott, 2013; Klein, 2015; Trottier, 2017; Loveluck, 2020). Their use of violence is seen as a tool to further their political ends, coupled with no direct means for controlling their activity, resulting in concerns that they represent a threat to society's stability and the state's monopoly on the use of violence. They have been condemned for wielding too much personal power, with no official practical or ethical oversight, and protected by a cloak of anonymity that only serves to further empower and embolden them. While, on the other hand, many of their causes – protecting people's freedom of expression, autonomy and privacy, balancing the power of the state, and fighting for LGBTQ+ rights – are intuitively good things to fight for (Ford, 2012; Littauer, 2013). Indeed, they have developed a political ethos that prioritizes protecting people from a variety of harms while furthering the value that cyberspace and the Internet can play in people's lives. They have been seen, therefore, to act to protect people – including from the state – when no other actors are able or willing to intervene.

This tension is further exacerbated by the significant disagreements across officials, media and laypeople regarding how hackers and the threat they represent should be understood and what place they could have in society. Throughout popular culture hackers have been referred to as 'heroes and hustlers, freedom fighters and cyber-lynch mobs, political activists and anarchists' (Klein, 2015: 379), and are often portrayed in media as 'lonely malicious criminals' (Thomas, 2002: 6). Part of this has included a significantly exaggerated state of fear across political elites from all branches of government as well as many members of the public. The framing used places them closer to the cyber-terrorist category than social progressive as a scandalized possibility of a hacker remotely taking over and crashing a plane or shutting down the electric power grid dominates the mindset regardless of either the feasibility or desire from hackers themselves (Gorman, 2012; Bamford, 2013). Even within academic literatures, political hackers are referred to as cyber-vigilantes (Trottier, 2017; Loveluck, 2020;), hacktivists (Denning, 1999; Mansfield-Devine, 2011a; Hampson, 2012; O'Malley, 2013; Goode, 2015) and cyber-terrorists (Padmanabhan, 2012), with significant overlap and slippage as to what label is applied to which hacker actor or activity. As a result, there is significant disagreement about what ethical role political hackers can, or should, have. Are they hiding in cyberspace, carrying out their private wars fuelled by personal beliefs and vendettas with no oversight or control, or are they a progressive force protecting people from harm when no one else can or will; do they have the right to use their technical skillset and cause destruction for their own political end, even under the banner of protecting people from harm; and, consequently, how should society respond to them exercising this power?

At its core this book will argue that political hacking can be justified when it is done to protect the vital interests of oneself or others. It is argued that all people have a fundamental interest in having their physical integrity, mental wellbeing, autonomy, liberty and privacy protected, and that they are of such importance that they create a duty on others not to violate them, while also empowering others to act in their defence when they are threatened. So vital are these interests that when they are under significant threat, and when traditional protectors (such as the state) are unwilling, unable or are the source of the threat, then non-state actors such as hackers can fill that space to offer that protection, and can even cause the threatening agent harm. Furthermore, it will be argued that providing this protection is more important than who carries it out. That is, just because hackers are outside the state does not automatically discount them as ethical actors and when the state fails to protect people – whether due to lack of ability, political will or negligence – hackers can fill the void. This will show that the state's monopoly on legitimate political violence is not incontestable and that non-state actors have the right to act when the state fails in its obligations to protect. Therefore, depending on the political end sought, the related political context, and the type of hacking operation utilized, the hacker can represent legitimate political actors and their actions can be justified.

The aim is not to inadvertently open the door to all private forms of political violence, nor is it to justify all hacking. The purpose of the ethical framework is to highlight the space for hackers to operate as legitimate actors; to guide hacker activity by detailing what actions are justified toward what end; to offer what mechanisms can be usefully created to aid in reaching these ethically justified decisions; and finally, to direct the political community on how to react, including when political hackers should be left alone as justified political actors, or located and punished for the unjustified harm they have caused. This means that the book will challenge those arguments that would discount hackers simply because they are acting outside the state's infrastructure and carrying out private forms of political violence, and will detail a more consistent framework for understanding what ethical hacking looks like.

What are 'political' hackers?

There is a significant degree of ambiguity surrounding both the broader hacker phenomenon and the more specific sub-set of political hacking. This is not surprising given the constantly evolving nature within hacking that is tied up with the changing personal history, political ideologies, targets and methods of a diverse hacker community. Indeed, the term hacking is loosely used to cover all forms of 'unauthorised access or use of a computer system', covering a range of different actors, intensions and activities (Conway, 2003: 10; see also Barber, 2001): from criminal hackers, or 'crackers', who maliciously attack or fraud systems for personal gain (Sheoran and Singh, 2014: 112); to 'Skript Kiddies', often young technologists who use hacking tools created by others to vandalize or disrupt the Internet (Farsole et al, 2010: 15); to hacktivists, a portmanteau of 'hacker' and 'activist' that use 'acts of civil disobedience and direct actions ... carried out in the virtual realm of the Internet' (Lowes, 2006: 115) to 'highlight political or social causes' (O'Malley, 2013: 140; see also Jordan and Taylor, 2004); to cyber-terrorists who use the Internet to further their objectives by causing significant damage in cyberspace or in the real world with the aim of promoting fear to a third party and damaging critical systems (Farsole et al, 2010: 15; see also Barber, 2001).

It is possible, therefore, to distinguish between those hacks that are motivated by some explicit political objective, as compared to financial or enjoyment purposes. A criminal hacker, or cracker, for instance, has the explicit aim of breaking into a system for profit through information blackmail, fraud or theft. For example, in 2016, Indian banks – including SBI, HDFC Bank, ICICI, YES Bank and Axis – had 3.2 million debit cards compromised in a hack (see Richmond, 2011). This is similar to the 2014 JPMorgan Chase data breach that was believed to have compromised the data associated with 83 million accounts (see Agrawal et al, 2014). While the WannaCry ransomware targeted computers running the Microsoft operating system and infected more than 230,000 computers in over 150 countries, locking people out of their computers until they paid the ransom (see McGoogan et al, 2017). Hacks for personal gain – often financial but can also be for reputation, renown or for destruction for its own sake – are therefore not being considered here. In the same way criminals and everyday non-political acts of violence can use similar methods and produce similar impacts, the context and ends sought mean that ethically they are fundamentally different to politically motivated violence.

Even looking at the more specific sub-set of political hacking, it can be difficult to categorize precisely what is being referred to and is something that is hotly debated. Gabriella Coleman, for example, argues that while hacker collectives like Anonymous are clearly political, they are also too fluid or 'rhizomatic', with too many influences that cause them to grow in different directions to attach any set ideology. Their self-defined 'anti-leader, anti-celebrity ethic' with operations 'open to all who care to contribute' has resulted in them engaging in a variety of political causes, from anti-piracy crusades, to securing online information rights against unjustified surveillance, to attacking Russia for its invasion of Ukraine in 2022 (Coleman, 2011: 511; see also Liu, 2004). In comparison, Greenberg argues that Anonymous does have an overarching political orientation where it 'attacks on whatever target offended its values, like freedom of speech and anti-corporatism' (Greenberg, 2012a: 183). Indeed, Fuchs, Golumbia and Levy all see Anonymous as reflecting core liberal ideologies, whether in the form of a socialist worldview or cyber-libertarianism, with a primary focus on free-speech, deregulation and meteoric sentiments (Levy, 1984; Borsook, 2000; Krauth, 2012; Fuchs, 2013; Golumbia, 2013). Steven Mansfield-Devine, on the other hand, argues that 'most Anons are driven by the desire for anarchic cyber-fun rather than any ideological conviction' (Mansfield-Devine, 2011a: 8). This labels hackers as different from having anarchism as a political ideology, but rather frames them as a destructive force gaining enjoyment out of chaos. This is not surprising as some hackers, most notably LulzSec, who pulled away from Anonymous, have wreaked havoc on major companies and agencies, including Sony, the US Public Broadcast Service, the *Sun* newspaper and government agencies like the FBI, CIA and the UK's Serious Crime Agency (Arthur, 2013), and have explicitly positioned themselves as acting to cause chaos for the fun of it, stating that 'if you want ethics go cry to Anonymous' in their Twitter Feed (Murphy, 2011: 47). According to their own media they had no higher purpose except the 'Lulz' or 'the pure joy of creating mayhem' (Mansfield-Devine, 2011a). While for Padmanabhan, hacking is nothing short of cyber-terrorism, in that while hackers did not seek to create a climate of fear, their methods and destruction amount to the same thing (Padmanabhan, 2012).

This lack of agreement is indicative of the wider challenge of trying to attach any single political agenda to hacking as a wider phenomenon or culture, as they evolve and move from one political debate to another. For example, looking across some of the most prominent political hackers in their relatively short history, the political agendas of hackers – whether individuals, groups with fixed, definable members or collectives with open and fluid membership[1] – have cut across nuclear disarmament,[2] government responses to local public disorders and protests,[3] government restrictions to online freedoms,[4] court decisions,[5] corruption, private actors restricting the sharing of information online (Coleman, 2014: 58, 121), organizing and facilitating public protests,[6] locating and revealing the identities of online-paedophiles and hate groups,[7] demonstrating the weakness and subsequent

---

[1]   Given the range of different compositions possible, 'hacker' and 'hackers' will be used as a generic means of referring to all forms – individual, group or collective – unless the organizational shape needs noting. 'Hacker/hackers' will therefore be taken as both a collective and singular noun.

[2]   In 1989 computers at NASA and the US Energy Department were hacked with the anti-nuclear 'WANK' worm, which altered login screens with the 'Worms Against Nuclear Killers' message, the second worm of its type used but the first with a distinctly political message (McCormick, 2000: 24).

[3]   Both Operation BART and Operation by Ferguson were Anonymous responding to the US officials restricting protests and review of police activity after the shooting of Charles Hill by the police in July 2011 and when police shot teenager Michael Brown (Stone, 2011; Rogers, 2014).

[4]   In 1990 the 'Cult of the Dead Cow' (cDc) worked (with the help of the Hong Kong Blondes, a groups cDc later stated they fabricated) to help Chinese citizens gain access to blocked websites (Menn, 2019; McCormick, 2000).

[5]   In April 2013, the suicide of Rehtaeh Parsons prompted Anonymous to action after they became aware of the failure of the Royal Canadian Mounted Police and Canadian officials to investigate a sexual assault (Coleman, 2014: 370).

[6]   For example, during the Arab Spring Operation Tunisia and Operation Egypt played an important role in the emerging protest movements by DDoS-ing government websites and helping dissidents circumvent online censorship (Emspak, 2011; Wagenseil, 2011).

[7]   Operation DeathEaters and Operation Darknet sought to collect evidence against international pedophile rings (Eleftheriou-Smith, 2015). Also from 2014 onwards Anonymous targeted the US hate group Klu Klux Klan, threatening to reveal the names of its members (O'Neil, 2015).

dangers of inadequate network security, and directly protesting and disrupting the growing power and prevalence of the security powers of the state.

It will be argued, however, that even across this extensive range of different political agendas, diverse set of hacker groupings, variety of tools used and hard to access phenomenological experiences, it is still possible to distinguish a set of hackers and hacking operations that are arguably distinctly, actively and purposefully political, with a nature that can be determined and described to form the basis of evaluating what possible ethical role they can possess. Indeed, in this way, political hackers are like any other set of actors in the wider tapestry of social movements, reacting, ebbing and flowing as the political landscape changes. To aid the discussion going forward, and despite this range of political issues that hackers have engaged in, there are still some persistent areas of concern that hackers coalesce around. This political agenda need not be definable as a single ideology, meaning it can shift and change over time from operation to operation. But what is key is that there is a distinguishable and notable political element that can be examined and evaluated to determine if and to what degree the political hacks are justified or not.

A method for evaluating a fluid collective

In order to be able to ethically evaluate this diverse and fluid set of political programmes, and especially for entities which embody a collective, anti-leader and secretive approach, this book will examine and map the hacking 'operation' as the focus of the hacker's activity and a manifestation of their political agenda. This will involve unpacking prominent hacking operations by detailing the methods employed, targets chosen, rhetoric given, damage allowed, political objectives and who is impacted, all of which are then placed in context of the wider political situation. This is useful as the operation is often the culmination of the internal dialogues and decisions of the hacker collective, and represents the outward presentation of the hacker's political role. This will include how operations evolve and change throughout their lifespan, and the different sub-phases involved to draw distinct ethical conclusions from the different aspects of the hacker's activity. In practice, the operations can vary greatly from the very specific efforts of an individual such as Aaron Swartz, who accessed and released academic papers from the JSTOR archives (Ludlow, 2013; Utterback, 2013), right through to large, open-ended and inclusive movements that span a longer timeframe with multiple strands, methods and targets involved, evolving and changing over their lifetime. For example, Anonymous's Operation Payback, which started as a retaliation hack when several Bollywood companies hired Aiplex Software to launch distributed denial of service (DDoS) attacks on piracy websites, quickly developed into a series of attacks on major pro-copyright and anti-piracy organizations, law firms and individuals, and then morphed into Operation Avenge Assange as a response to the banks who had withdrawn banking facilities from WikiLeaks (Coleman, 2014: 96–105). This reflects not only the quick turn an operation can take but also how different parts of an operation can receive individual ethical justification or condemnation.

Unpacking and detailing the operations in this way also allows for an evaluation of the main political impact of a hack without becoming distracted by the hackers' individual, internal personal agendas, especially given the fluid and difficult-to-detail membership. Indeed, it could be that some members are involved because of their genuine belief in the stated political agenda of the collective, while others might contribute because of some other general belief (anti-establishmentism, for example), whereas some might wish to feel a sense of inclusion and camaraderie and so contribute, and some might act to demonstrate their power and influence. However, in such an open situation, it is both unhelpful and unnecessary to examine the intentions and motivations of all the individuals involved if they all contribute towards the same ends, through the same means, with the same limitations.[8] This approach is similar to ethical methods that involve evaluating fluid political entities or collectives which are pursuing long-term political agendas through multi-streamed approaches, but where it is still possible to make both categorizations and distinctions in terms of their aims, methods and key actors, and then ethically condone or condemn different aspects over others. For example, when evaluating a state's decision to go to war and the subsequent performance in that war, it is possible to simultaneously judge the state's activities as a collective endeavour while also breaking down various aspects to make specific statements on the leadership, soldiers, individuals and political community. Indeed, even when various individuals work towards a common goal while following the same methods yet for very different personal reasons, it is still possible to isolate an overriding political agenda as well as the ringleaders (politicians and commanders in the war-time example) who must represent and take responsibility of the super-organisms operational behaviour (see Sankowski, 1992: 291–9; Williams, 2003; Braham and van Hees, 2012: 601–34; Lepora and Goodin, 2013; Bellaby, 2018: 574–602).

In practice, therefore, even within the most fluid of collectives where multiple voices are calling for a variety of different political agendas, it is still

---

[8]   For a flexible methodology on tracking and distributing responsibility across complex relationships and within fluid collectives see Bellaby, who argues for a fluid and flexible understanding on the different normative roles various actors play which in turn can shape the type and level of responsibility allocated, and subsequently the specific type of punishment required (Bellaby, 2018: 574–602).

possible to see a 'shared awareness', where 'otherwise uncoordinated groups begin to work together' and act towards a common goal (Shirky, 2008: 163). The so-called 'hive-mind' of Anonymous, for example, operates as a super-organism, with many individuals working individually but possessing the nature of a single entity, and outwardly expressing a significantly coherent political rationale and narrative as a result. This is particularly important and helpful in evaluating the actions of those operations that necessarily rely on a wide and open involvement from the hacker community. For example, *en masse* methods such as DDoS attacks, virtual sit-ins and email bombs can utilize thousands of individuals contributing to the effort. In this instance, the political agenda and actions of the collective are examined through the operation rather than any given individual.

Equally important, this mapping allows one to determine whether the actions truly reflect the hacker's stated political intent and are not being used as a cover for private gain, whether financial or reputational. By looking across the stated political agendas of the hackers and connecting them to the methods, targets, narratives and stated ends, it is possible to understand if and how they (in)congruently match each other in the operation. For example, if the justification is one of self-defence, then the actions must flow directly from this and not involve tactics of domination or subjugation. We can track back from the methods and circumstances of a situation to understand the intention.

Positioning the debate

This book builds on the essential works and ideas from across a range of literatures that examine hacking as a technological, cultural, political and legal phenomenon. One set of works that are not necessarily explored here, but are still worth noting, are those that look at the use and justification of corporate 'white hat' or 'grey hat' hackers: people who test computer networks for weaknesses, with the former testing with the owner's permission and the latter informing the owner after the fault has been found.[9] The aim of these hackers is to determine what system an intruder can access and what information can be collected, what they can do with the available information, and whether anyone at the target system has noticed the hack (Sheoran and Singh, 2014: 113). This body of work examines whether such uninvited activity should be encouraged or trusted when there is no mechanism for directing or controlling what such individuals do (see Farsole et al, 2010; Cardwell, 2011; Bansal and Arora 2012; Lu, 2015). These hacker

---

[9] For example, 'World of Hell' was a grey hat computer hacker attack specialized in targeting websites with poor security and defacing them with an advice message.

activities are often of direct corporate interest, where the weaknesses found are purposefully remedied to increase overall security. The hacking explored here, however, looks at politically or socially motivated hacking where the use of violence is both necessary and a direct means for furthering the hackers' political ends.

Another set of interesting debates outside of this book is the growing work on state cyber warfare. That is, what happens when states use cyberspace to attack another state, either directly through the shutting down of critical infrastructures or through subversive manipulation of media and propaganda, industrial espionage or financial manipulations. The Stuxnet computer worm, for example, found in computers at Iran's Natanz nuclear site landed a significant blow on any Iranian nuclear ambitions without anyone lifting a sword (Farwell and Rohozinski, 2011: 24–5; Sanger, 2012). Similarly, cyber-attacks on civilian structures, such as the case in Estonia in 2007, which brought down the websites of its banks, governmental agencies and media outlets, demonstrated the vulnerability of such structures as well as their increased importance in the modern world (BBC News, 2007; Blomfield, 2007; Landler and Markoff, 2007; Traynor, 2007). Equally important is the threat of cyber-espionage. 'Titan Rain', for example, stole data from NASA's Mars Reconnaissance Orbiter and Air Force flight planning software as well as data from US government systems and defence contractors (Sommer and Brown, 2011; Posner, 2017); 'Operation Aurora' consisted of numerous attacks on high-tech, security and defence contractor companies (Cha and Nakashima, 2010); and Operation 'Ghostnet' accessed the foreign affairs ministries of Iran, Indonesia and the Philippines and the embassies of India, South Korea, Indonesia, Thailand and Taiwan as well as computers at NATO headquarters (Information Warfare Monitor, 2009). The academic work within this field examines if and how conceptualizations of interstate warfare can accommodate this move to cyberspace and the impact it is likely to have on international relations. The focus of this study, however, will be on private as compared to state or state-sponsored hackers, and these can range from lone-wolf individuals, to small-fixed-membership groups, to loosely defined, mutable and leaderless collectives, and whose targets can include state infrastructure and state representatives, private corporations and private individuals, or even other hackers.

Moreover, this book rests and builds on three important academic areas and assumptions. First is the broader work on the ethics of defensive harm, and to some extent the debates found within the just war tradition. As stated previously, the ethical underpinning of the book's argument is one of justifying harming another in self-defence or defence of another when vital interests are under threat. This, firstly, draws on Martha Nussbaum and Joel Fienberg's conceptualization of harm: that through a notion of overlapping consensuses, vital interests held by all individuals can be established 'without accepting any particular metaphysical conception of the world, any particular comprehensive ethical or religious view, or even any particular view of the person or human nature' (Nussbaum, 2000: 76). Quite simply, an individual's core interests can be determined by isolating those aspects of the human condition where, if the quality were to fall below a threshold level, the individual would cease to be considered to be living as 'truly human, that is, *worthy* of a human being' (Nussbaum, 2000: 73). On the other side of this coin is then the work on defensive harm, including Cecile Fabre's work as well as the key ethical underpinnings found in the just war tradition most broadly (see McMahan, 1994; Walzer, 2000; McMahan, 2006; Fabre, 2008; Fabre, 2012; Bellaby 2014; Bellaby, 2016; Fabre, 2018; Pattison 2018). This is not a direct application of the widely stated version of the just war tradition onto hacking, as there are too many incongruities. But as will become apparent in Chapter 2, there are some clear synergies with the underlying ethical arguments found within the tradition: most notably, the need for a clear justifying reason, often based on self-defence; the importance of distinguishing between legitimate and illegitimate targets so only those who 'deserve' the negative impact receive it; the role that right intention has in preventing abuse of the ethical criteria for subversive private interests; and the importance of authority, and recent works around the question of non-state actors claiming the right to engage in armed resistance against occupation or domestic tyranny.

Secondly, this book will draw heavily on the sociological and anthropological work on hackers as entities engaging in a specific set of cultural, social and political activities. This includes a significant focus on Anonymous in many of the case examples as it has played a prominent role in the public space with some of the most reported and arguably politically significant hacks. Anonymous also raises some interesting questions given its fluid membership and the impact this can have on its changing focus and political agenda. However, there will also be engagement with Telecomix, a group notable for their commitment to freedom of expression; Phineas Phisher, which targets surveillance companies with a general leftist-anarchist mantra; and individuals such as Aaron Swartz and Jeremy Hammond. This body of work offers a valuable insight into what hackers are doing, their own stated reasons, and how they operate, especially in terms of how they function within a leaderless, brand-orientated organizational structure. Most prominent within this field is Gabriella Coleman's whole body of work, but specifically *Hacker, Hoaxer, Whistleblower, Spy: The Many Faces of Anonymous* (Coleman, 2014). Having gained exclusive access to Anonymous members via online forums and interviews, Coleman gives an inside knowledge of what was happening across some of the most significant Anonymous hacks, providing a pivotal insight into hacker practices, policies, personalities and mentalities. Similarly, Joseph Menn's *Cult of the Dead Cow: How the Original*

Hacking Supergroup Might Save the World offers a useful and detailed account of the Cult of the Dead Cow hacker collective by tracking and detailing their historical development (Menn, 2019). Finally, Molly Sauter's *The Coming Swarm: DDoS Actions, Hacktivism and Civil Disobedience on the Internet* looks specifically at the practice of DDoS actions as a tactic of political activism and the impact that it has on society (Sauter, 2015). The contribution of these bodies of work is that they provide an insight into the mentality and activities of the hackers themselves.

Finally, this book will further those works that seek to determine whether hacking is a justifiable act of (violent) political activism or not. Looking across the literature, political hacking has broadly been referred to as digital resistance (Delmas, 2018a), digital disobedience (Scheuerman, 2016), or digital activism (Sauter, 2015), though of the various definitions one of the most often used is 'hacktivism'. The natural attraction of hacktivism arises from its literal portmanteau of 'hack' and 'activism', highlighting the aim of bringing about social or political change through cyber-activity while also emphasizing its socially progressive elements. By associating hacking with political activism, it provides civil disobedience as an evaluative framework, offering established avenues for judging political hacking by associating it with recognized forms of political participation. For example, Kenneth Himma argues that hacktivism is 'the commission of an unauthorised digital intrusion for the purpose of expressing a political or moral position' and is 'nonviolent in nature' (Himma, 2008: 200). Candice Delmas describes hacktivism as involving acts that are a 'public, non-violent, politically motivated, and conscientious breach of law undertaken with the aim of bringing about a change in laws or government policies' (Delmas, 2018a: 65), while others emphasize the 'peaceful breaking of unjust laws' with 'non-violent means to expose wrongs, raise awareness, and prohibit the information on perceived unethical laws by individual, organisations, companies or governments' (Manion and Goodrum, 2000: 14; see also Dittrich and Himma, 2006: Taylor and Harris, 2006; Hampson, 2012; Goode, 2015; Crosston, 2017; Alexopoulou and Pavli, 2019). Indeed, Cult of the Dead Cow's Oxblood Ruffin defined hacktivism as something that uses 'technology to improve human rights. It also employs non-violent tactics and is aligned with the original intent of the Internet, which is to keep things up and running' (Smallridge et al, 2016: 61). Furthermore, Delmas notes that 'painting hacktivism as civil disobedience highlights their principles and communicative intentions' where their actions are 'speech acts, grounded in sincere political commitments', situating it to the 'broader public as a protest' and therefore well within the 'respectable tradition of civil disobedience' (Delmas, 2018a: 64; see also Auty, 2004; Hampson, 2012; Jordan, 2014).

Analogies are therefore often made between the real-world, non-violent activist activities and how they become manifested in the cyber-realm

(Hampson, 2012). For example, plastering graffiti across a building with a political message is akin to website defacement, while blocking a particular building's main thoroughfare through a public sit-in becomes a 'virtual sit-in' where individuals *en masse* request information from a website's server, resulting in a bottleneck that prevents other people from accessing the information. Barricades become website redirects whereby the hacker makes an unauthorized change to the targeted website's Internet address on the Domain Name Service so that when people try to access one site they are redirected to a site of the hacker's choosing. And political theatre is meme distribution (Denning, 1999; Wiemann, 2004; Crosston, 2017). The Electrohippies, for example, argued for this natural synergy between real-world and cyberspace protest methods: 'the same principles of traditional civil disobedience, like trespass and blockage, will still be applied but more and more these acts will take place in electronic or digital form' (Fitri, 2011: 9). Such appeals have a clear heritage, starting in 1998 with Electronic Disturbance Theatre running a series of virtual sit-ins, first against the Mexican President Zedillo's website and later against President Clinton's White House website, the Pentagon, the Frankfurt stock exchange, and the Mexican stock exchange. The aim is to 'call attention to the protesters and their causes by disrupting normal operations and blocking facilities' (Denning, 1999: 6). Similarly, Strano Network used virtual sit-ins against the French government to highlight policies on nuclear weapons and social issues (Denning, 1999). Like their real-world counterparts these actions were mainly focused on being an act of protest in and of themselves, performed as 'a call to public attention' to a particular issue through the act of 'disruption of the normal operation of a victim site and denying or preventing access to the site' (Kizza, 2020: 115). The messaging in these cases was the key aim of the hack.

The justification of 'hacktivism' is therefore akin to civil disobedience 'in so far as it is permissible to stage sit-ins in a commercial or government building to protest laws that violate human rights, it is permissible to intrude … on networks' in a similar fashion (Himma, 2005: 1). Importantly, civil disobedience's long intellectual history has been one of non-violence. It is argued that in 'nearly just societies' resisting a law is only civil disobedience when it is public, non-violent and is a conscientious breach of law undertaken to bring about a change in laws or government policies (Rawls, 2009; see also Martin, 1970; Manion and Goodrum, 2000; Dittrich and Himma, 2006; Taylor and Harris, 2006; Hampson, 2012; Goode, 2015; Crosston, 2017; Alexopoulou and Pavli, 2019). It 'does not condone violent or destructive acts against its enemies, focusing instead on nonviolent means to expose wrongs, raise awareness, and prohibit the implementation of perceived unethical laws by individuals, organizations, corporations or governments' (Manion and Goodrum, 2000: 14). It is the 'principled and deliberate breach of law intended to protest unjust laws, politics, institutions, or practices and undertaken by agents broadly committed to basic norms of civility' (Delmas, 2018b: 17); or the conscientious and communicative breach of law designed to demonstrate condemnation to direct a change in law, through non-violent means with a willingness to accept the consequences (Brownlee, 2012: 18). In all of these definitions non-violence sits at the centre of civil disobedience.

However, it will be argued in Chapter 1 that contemporary hacks go beyond this conceptualization of hacktivism. While a key messaging and protest element is still involved, the hacks are also directly working to change a policy or decision through coercive force and direct action. The use of political violence is both an inherent aspect of many of the tools utilized by the hackers as well as a critical feature for trying to force change. Chapter 1 will detail how the use of DDoS attacks, doxxing, leaks, and viruses and malware by contemporary political hackers necessarily uses coercive power or damage, and therefore political violence, and are powerful as a result. Furthermore, this political hacking has often necessarily involved the practice of covert activity, running counter to many justified conceptualizations of civil disobedience that require publicity (Brownlee, 2016). Framing political hacking as a form of civil disobedience ignores actions that necessarily involve political violence but which could still be potentially justifiable. This violence needs its own evaluation that considers the ends to which it is being used rather than be automatically discounted. The violence is necessary and important.

It will therefore be argued that the damage or disruption caused by the political hack is a necessary mechanism for both disseminating a message and drawing attention to the underlying political principle, as well as the attack acting as a direct means of affecting change against the source of the problem. This places it closer to Candice Delmas' work on 'uncivil disobedience' as an activity where the acts are 'covert, evasive, violent, or offensive' (Delmas, 2018b: 47). Delmas' work is valuable as it looks at those actions often discounted simply by being 'uncivil' and engages with those who denounce such activity due to obedience to the law, harm to democracy and the need for social stability. Delmas broadly argues that, along with others such as Celikates and Roberts, 'There is a place for uncivil disobedience in liberal democratic societies when ... some citizens are effectively (de facto but not de jure) denied full and equal status; and the injustice of this denial is not publicly recognized, perhaps because that injustice is not deliberate but results from the interplay of social practices and institutional structures, as in cases of structural injustice' (Delmas, 2018b: 64; see also Celikates, 2015). That is, when the system is so hardwired against providing the same justices as everyone else is benefiting from, not only is there a right but a duty to use uncivil means to fight it: 'justified on the (broadly liberal and democratic) grounds that they contribute to advancing justice and democracy, by jolting the public into recognizing pressing claims of oppression' (Delmas, 2018b: 67). This label of uncivil disobedience synergizes and energizes the argument put forward here by pushing for a set of justifiable political activist actions that can use violence as part of their arsenal. What this book advances on is drawing out the underlying ethical justification beyond the reliance on liberal, democratic political civic friendship and for a universal and fundamental right to self-defence and defence of others, even when that act of self-defence can cause others significant harm. As a result, the ethical framework argued here provides for a greater range of political actions beyond even uncivil disobedience (Delmas, 2018b: 48).

Structure

In order to create this ethical framework, Chapter 1 will provide special attention to the nature of political hacking as exemplified by collectives such as Anonymous, detailing how to understand both the nature of political hacking as well as why it necessarily utilizes political violence, and why understanding that violence is a pivotal part of determining its ethical quality. Chapter 1 will argue, therefore, that the methods chosen by political hackers necessarily rely on the use of political violence, which separates it from acts of activism and civil disobedience, and that the violence inflicted occurs at varying levels depending on the means, targets and ends chosen. This will involve unpacking what it means to cause political violence, arguing that it is possible to create a spectrum across which different political acts can be placed depending on the level and type of harm or destruction they cause. It will argue that by conceptualizing political violence as a spectrum the different hacks can be spread across it. This will allow a similar spread in Chapter 2, which will outline the ethical framework for evaluating political hacking. Chapter 2 will argue that when hacking is done to protect people from harm, the subsequent damage or harms the hackers cause can be justified. Chapter 2 will also argue that hackers can be understood as legitimate users of political violence as they act to prevent harm to people as a form of defending others, while also outlining that as the level of damage to be caused by the political hack goes up, so should the threat they are defending again. This will also include essential decision-making processes needed to limit personal bias and other additional limitations to ensure that the correct means are used against the right people. This combined ethical framework will be applied to the case study chapters, with Chapter 3 examining operations whose objectives are focused on protecting the online manifestations of people's autonomy, liberty and privacy, especially in terms of their role in facilitating people's 'political autonomy'. Chapter 4 will explore the ethical value of hackers enabling the leaking of private information depending on, firstly, whether it reveals wrongdoing and the extent of that wrongdoing, and secondly, the public's right to be informed explicitly about what was being hidden. In comparison, Chapter 5 will look at the expansion of the hacker mandate to cases beyond information rights and to issues such as police brutality, the failure of due and fair process, the creation of laws that seek to directly discriminate and foster hatred and violence against members of the LGBTQ+ community, and the failure to locate and punish online paedophiles. Chapter 6 will return to the ethical framework to offer guidance on how society should react to such activity, arguing for an update to the existing law as well as how such political hacking should be understood.

1

Hacks, Hackers and Political Hacking

Introduction

The rise of the political-hacker phenomenon over the last two decades is something distinctive from instances of simple boasting, ransomware hijackers making money, or chaos creating malcontents. Part of this distinctiveness is both the political agenda these hackers have come to possess, as well as the necessary use of violence as part of them furthering their political end. Importantly, however, the form of this violence, level of negative impact inflicted and the type of targets chosen can all vary dramatically across operations, which can shape whether or not the hack can be justified. Therefore, this chapter will outline a spectrum of political violence, arguing that depending on what the target is, and how and to what extent it is negatively impacted, as well as the associated political context, the level of violence can vary. This will allow different hacks to be placed across a spectrum of political violence. This will enable Chapter 2 to develop a similar spectrum of justification that can determine if and when a particular activity or operation is justified, given the level of violence used compared to the ends and political context. This spectrum approach allows for the diverse set of hacking operations to be examined in greater depth, detailing the political objectives the hackers work towards, the methods used, and those who are impacted and in what ways. This will enable a better understanding of what politically motivated hacking looks like and how the highly varied actions used by hackers can compare and receive different justifications or denouncements according to the situation.

The evolving history of hacking and the birth of a political Anonymous

Online rights and freedoms

Historically, the broad hacker culture finds its origins in the 1950s within MIT's student organization 'Tech Model Railroad Club' – a group of students who shared a passion for understanding how things worked that naturally developed into the intellectual challenge of creatively overcoming the limitations of software systems to achieve novel and clever outcomes. Though initially driven by technical curiosity, over the following decades hackers started to use their skills to promote their own political beliefs and agendas (Levy, 1984). These first-generation hackers were broadly motivated by pro-freedom of information, anti-authoritarian, anti-nuclear and anti-capitalist sentiments, with many of these ideals still being pertinent in today's modern hackers. For example, in 1989, computers at NASA and the US Energy Department were hacked with the anti-nuclear 'WANK' worm, which altered login screens with the 'Worms Against Nuclear Killers' message, the second worm of its type used but the first with a distinctly political message (McCormick, 2013). Following this, in 1990, the 'Cult of the Dead Cow' (cDc) worked (with the help of the Hong Kong Blondes, a group cDc later stated they fabricated) to help Chinese citizens gain access to blocked websites (Menn, 2019: 115); in 1994 the 'Zippies' launched an email bomb and DDoS attack against the British government over the Criminal Justice Public Order Act which sought to ban raves with music containing a 'succession of repetitive beats'; in 1996 the Department of Justice website was changed to the Department of *In*justice; and in 1998 Legions of the Underground declared war again Iraq and China and aimed to bring down their Internet access (McCormick, 2013).

However, these initial political hacks were relatively small in size and ran under the mainstream media radar. It was not until the age of Anonymous that hacking would really gain popular attention and become globally recognized. Born in the *4Chan* forums – an online anonymous English-language imageboard founded by Christopher Poole in 2003, whose purpose was to provide a space for users to share images and create threaded discussions on any topic, all done anonymously – users congregated around the desire for the freedom that such anonymity provided them. These forums started as a melting pot of ideas that allowed people to gravitate around shared beliefs and whose anonymity enabled people to congregate *en masse* to carry out online pranks and raids. At this point Anonymous became a name 'synonymous with trolling: an activity that seeks to ruin the reputations of individuals and organisations and reveal embarrassing and personal information' (Coleman, 2014: 4).

However, while the origins of Anonymous are founded in trolling, causing mischief and mayhem for its own sake, in 2008 the collective made a significant reorientation that would lay out its political intentions and shape its future, shifting away from '"coordinated motherfuckery"' to 'earnest activist endeavour' (Coleman, 2014: 4). After an online leaked video where Tom Cruise, a well-known member of the Church of Scientology, expressed his 'enthused ... devotion' (Norton, 2012) to this particular church was taken down off the Internet, members of the online community congregating around the Anonymous identity saw this as an attempt to censor the Internet, flying directly against the importance they placed on online freedoms. In response, Project Chanology was born: members of Anonymous, known as Anons, carried out several cyber-related attacks, which included launching 'DDoS attacks on Scientology websites', ordering 'unpaid pizzas and escorts to Scientology churches across North America', faxing 'images of nude body parts' and barraging phone lines with prank calls (Coleman, 2014: 58). The attack soon gained notoriety, being picked up by widespread media who prominently displayed the Guy Fawkes masks, quickly entrenching this as a symbol that would come to globally represent the Anonymous brand (Coleman, 2014: 67). This marked the first step along a more purposeful and political endeavour: 'Trolling had given way to an earnest activist endeavour, as if Anonymous had emerged from its online sanctuary and set out to improve the world' (Coleman, 2014: 6).

Following the early success and notoriety of Operation Chanology, Anonymous continued with several prominent cases, including giving its support to WikiLeaks in Operation Avenge Assange after the organization's money flow was halted by PayPal, Mastercard and Visa, as well as a series of operations in Tunisia, Egypt, Iran, the Philippines and Thailand, arguing in each case for the vital importance of online freedoms and access to information. Indeed, Operation Chanology had represented the beginning of the shift towards a brand centred on a core belief in online freedoms, with a 'sizable portion of Anons now firmly committed to this politically engaged style of hacking', representing a move away from trolling and pranking for the simple sake of it (Coleman, 2014: 73). This became increasingly evident in the public rhetoric, persona, iconography and political-social beliefs that shaped their political mission, targets, methods and justifications.

Despite a clear political shift, however, this early ethos does not amount to a clear-cut set of political principles articulated in a singular and unifying fashion. Instead, it is a broad set of priorities reflective of Steven Levy's early work on the 'hacker ethic' – many of which still underpin much of modern political hacking. These principles include: that access to cyberspace should be 'unlimited and total'; that 'all information should be free'; that hackers should 'mistrust authority – promote decentralization'; with an objective to 'create art and beauty on a computer'; and that 'computers can change your life for the better' (metac0m, 2003). These underlying principles can be seen to play a pivotal part in much of the political hacker's agenda, cutting across time, hackers and activists: from the Electronic Disturbance Theatre and Critical Art Essembled, who use cyber-activism to explore and trumpet the 'intersections between art, critical theory, technology, and political activism' (Critical Art Ensemble, 1996; Wray, 1999); to whistleblowers Manning and Snowden, who release national security secrets under the argument of the public's right to know; to organizations such as the Electronic Frontier Foundation, an international non-profit digital rights group who 'champions user privacy, free expression, and innovation through impact litigation, policy analysis, grassroots activism, and technology development' (Electronic Frontier Foundation, http://www.eff.org); to grassroots actions of 'millions of people who download pirated movies and music from torrent websites like The Pirate Bay'; to causes and movements such as 'net neutrality', which argues that the Internet should treat all users equally and not discriminate based on the user, content or, most significantly, based on the costs individuals or organizations are willing to pay.

This prioritization of information freedoms, both online and in the real world, came to act as the core of Anonymous's political agenda, clearly articulated early on in its political reorientation. In a video released in 2011 Anonymous announced to the world:

> Hello Internet. I am one Anonymous. Anonymous is a collective of individuals united by an awareness here to promote the truth, promote free speech, stand up against human injustice, we fight corrupt corporations and protest governments who bastardise freedom. (FLSnag, 2011)

These ideas were then further reflected in its 2011 'Anonymous Manifesto', stating that:

- a society must be allowed to share information unrestrained and uncensored if it is to maintain cultural and technological revolution, and uphold the rights and liberties of its citizens;
- citizens must be allowed to organise their own institutions without being harassed by existing institutions privileged by greater resources, influence and power; that members of the public must be free to circulate uncensored information in order to guarantee their rights;
- these rights are violated when a more powerful institution, such as the law or government, unfairly uses its sway to disband or harass citizen organisations; citizens should not be the target of any undue surveillance;

- privacy and secrecy are privileges granted to the institutions built by citizens and their communities, as long as the institution does not utilise that secrecy to deceive or act against the common interests of humanity;
- it is the responsibility of all citizens to take actions and maintain an open and transparent society. (Anonymous, 2011)

Oversight and transparency

A companion to this focus on online rights is a corresponding belief in the need to 'mistrust authority', arguing that power – both state and private – can represent a significant threat to individuals, minorities, social groups and society itself. As a result, hackers have expressed strong anti-establishment, anti-state or libertarian sentiments (Fuchs, 2013). This is the decentralization argument, where the best way to promote the free exchange of information is to have an open system with no boundaries and where authorities – governments, bureaucracies and corporate actors – are flawed systems that represent a threat to people's interests, as they naturally place limits on what people can do. Indeed, David Golumbia argues that Anonymous is a 'cyber-libertarian entity' with a consistent philosophy that the Internet should be free from government regulation (Golumbia, 2013; see also Boorsook, 2000; Naughton, 2000; Goode 2015). This means endorsing both a negative conception of freedom where all constraints and limitations are removed as well as positive freedoms with government policies placing enabling and universal access requirements on telecom companies (Golumbia, 2013). This feeds strongly into the importance hackers place on transparency and anti-corruption, with an especially 'high level of transparency from governments and corporate elite', underpinning a general endorsement of whistleblowers and sharing platforms such as WikiLeaks with their work to collect and disclose 'secretive information that from the perspective of the Anons ought to have been free' (Serracino-Inglott, 2013). Part of this includes a 'right to know' that emphasizes transparency in government activities, especially in the national security arena.

Beyond information freedoms

As political hacking has gained momentum, hacker collectives like Anonymous have widened the realm of what political threats they are interested in defending against. This has included taking an aggressive stance against terrorist organization ISIS following the terrorist attack in Paris in 2015 that killed 12 and injured 11 others, with Anonymous devoting itself to locating and rooting out the social media accounts of ISIS supporters. Its efforts were subsequently ramped up following the ISIS Paris attacks on 13 November 2015, with Anonymous declaring war against ISIS (Hern,

2015). While in both Nigeria and Uganda, Anonymous launched hacker attacks against the government in response to their anti-LGBTQ+ legislation that expressed the 'intent to pass a law that would jail LGBT people for up to 14 years' along with other discriminatory policies (Littauer, 2013; see also Brocklebank, 2012). Then, through Operation DeathEaters and Operation Dark Net, hackers sought to collect evidence against international paedophile rings so as to 'bring them to justice'. Anonymous reported that 'The Westminster paedophile ring is one of many cases where Operation DeathEaters has actively pursued and sought truth, in order to end the hideous crimes concealed behind the British elite' (Eleftheriou-Smith, 2015).

In Operation BART, Operation Ferguson and an operation in Cleveland, Anonymous aided the protest movements that were being held in response to the fatal shooting by police of Charles Hill, Michael Brown and 12-year-old Temir Rice, respectively, supporting not only the actual protests themselves but using hacks to directly attack the police in order to force a public investigation, as the protesters felt officials did not sufficiently follow up the incidents (Rogers, 2014; RT.Com, 2014; Stone, 2014).

These operations demonstrate a widening of Anonymous's political agenda, away from purely freedom of information or online freedom causes and more towards issues where people had been or were likely to be harmed, especially when the usual systems failed to offer the necessary protections. In these cases, the attacks were directed against agents in power where hackers used their coercive influence to attack the state either when it has failed in its duty to protect society or when it becomes a direct threat to society.

A political violence spectrum

These various cases show that hackers have a vast landscape of political interests. Importantly, many of the operations necessarily use violence to achieve those political ends. However, before this can be made clear in terms of political hacking, it is first necessary to outline what political violence means and how it can be conceptualized as a spectrum.

At its simplest and broadest, political violence is the use of violence for political purposes, goals, motivations or to engender political repercussions. As a term, concept or description, political violence is widely used and covers a range of very diverse activities and instances, with many of the existing definitions gravitating towards being 'all-inclusive rather than precise' in their form. Donatella della Porta outlines the broad understanding of political violence as 'collective action that involves great physical force and causes damage to an adversary in order to impose political aims', which then branches out from here to cover a large range of political activities (Della Porta, 1995: 2). From, 'armed revolution, civil strife, terrorism, war, and other such causes that can result in injury or loss of property', to 'terrorism, rebellion, war, conquest, revolution, oppression, tyranny, and many others' (Darby, 2016: 17), to mass protests, coups, terrorism, riots, pograms, ethnic cleansing and genocide. Notably, these lists focus on the more destructive forms of political violence and are not easily translatable to many of the types of violence carried out by political hackers. There is a need, therefore, for a clearer understanding and differentiation between acts or circumstances of political violence at the lower end.

Harms and damages

To start with, a key defining feature of political violence is its negative impact – the harm or damage that it causes. This is more than a tautological statement outlining that political violence is violent, but rather argues that it is important to understand specifically what is being negatively impacted, to what level, how often and in what way. Depending on the negative impact involved, not only does the conceptualization of the violence change but so too does its understanding as a political act. Some definitions of political violence take this impact very broadly, such as John Dewey's, which argues that violence is force gone wrong, that 'energy becomes violence when it defeats or frustrates purposes instead of executing or realizing it' (Dewey, 1980: 246). This creates an encompassing understanding but offers little detail that is helpful in the ethical evaluation. Other conceptualizations, however, focus on its physical aspects and the direct impact it can have on individuals. For example, Thomas Pogge states that 'a person uses physical violence if he acts in a way that blocks another's exercise of her legitimate claim rights by physical means' (Pogge, 1991: 67), while for Manfred Steger 'violence is the intentional infliction of physical or psychological injury' (Steger, 2003: 13). And others refer to violence in terms of a violation, 'to infringe, transgress or exceed some limit or norm' (Bufacchi, 2005: 196).

In order to add more detail and nuance to these broad categorizations it is necessary to draw out the distinction between causing harm and causing damage, as well as how both can occur to varying degrees. That is, to cause harm refers to the negative impact that befalls our core needs or requirements, our vital interests. This conceptualization of harm runs throughout the book and begins with the realization that individuals have certain requirements that are both 'vital' to them and vulnerable to outside interference. Joel Feinberg argues that individuals have a set of interests that form the prerequisites or preconditions that must exist if they are to fulfil their more ultimate life goals. Feinberg calls these requirements 'welfare interests', and John Rawls calls them 'primary goods', but essentially they both amount to the same thing, that is, regardless of what conception of the good life the individual holds or what his life plans might be in detail, these preconditions must be satisfied first in order to achieve them (Rawls,

1971: 62; Feinberg, 1984: 37). Martha Nussbaum argues that through a notion of overlapping consensuses core vital interests held by all individuals can be established 'without accepting any particular metaphysical conception of the world, any particular comprehensive ethical or religious view, or even any particular view of the person or human nature' (Nussbaum, 2000: 76). Quite simply, an individual's core interests can be determined by isolating those aspects of the human condition where, if the quality were to fall below a threshold level, the individual would cease to be considered to be living as 'truly human, that is, *worthy* of a human being' (Nussbaum, 2000: 73). For example, being creatures of flesh and bone instantly 'implies mortality, vulnerability and agency' (Butler, 2004: 26), demonstrating the need to protect the physical body as one of our most important vital interests. But protecting the physical body is not all. The need for mental integrity, autonomy, liberty and a degree of privacy are each vital in an individual's life and thus need protecting. If these vital interests fall below a threshold level, the ability to realize more ultimate needs, goals or activities can become dramatically hindered. In this way, these interests can be recognized and conceptualized as the most important interests a person has, inherent features of the human condition that necessarily cry out for protection. 'Harm', therefore, can quite simply be defined as the violation of an individual's most vital interests. These interests have intrinsic value and damaging them can cause harm regardless of the repercussions. Even if, on balance, the individual does not experience the harm in a 'tangible and material' way, they can still be said to be harmed since their vital interests have been violated or wronged (Feinberg, 1984: 35). This understanding of vital interests is the source of many of the legal and normative rights, duties and liberties that exist as they seek to protect, provide or further our core vital interests. To cause harm, therefore, means to violate these vital interests, and through this conceptualization a greater understanding of the nature of political violence can be achieved. For example, violence can include attacks that violate people's vital interests, such as physical attacks on their body, physiological attacks on their emotional state or psyche, restricting their physical liberty, manipulating or unduly influencing their ability to make their own decisions or exercise their autonomy, or impinging or removing their privacy.

Political violence as damage, in comparison, is much broader in its framing of the negative impact caused. This can include, for example, the damage caused to people's secondary pursuits as well as the negative impact to material and non-material entities such as buildings, finances, infrastructure, reputation, property, resources, time or livelihood. For example, loss of earnings, damage to property and loss of reputation are all important negative impacts and can be 'felt' by more than just individuals, but are distinct from harm caused by the violation of our vital interests. This is not to say that causing harm is necessarily worse than damaging something as both can vary in the level of negative impact, and in some instances one might be considered as more negative than the other. What this distinction does is to give detail and understanding to the nature of the political act. What is violated or damaged, therefore, sits at the core of understanding the type of political violence involved.

Intent, motivation and context

Following this, the political context, intent and end sought can give shape to the political nature of the violence. Again, this will help the classification and the broader understanding of the political violence and subsequent political, social or ethical justifications. Different examples of motivation or intent might include justice, protecting others, self-defence, profit, reparations, political statements, self-expression, raising awareness and providing for or protecting rights. Or they could include punishment, control, intimidation, subjugation, coercion, agenda-setting, domination, marginalization and the maintenance of existing power dynamics. For example, the state's use of violence could come in the form of imprisonment or capital punishment and could be motivated by the intent to carry out (retributive) justice, or it could be to enforce a political belief, policy or plan, religious code, or to maintain the existing political order. Similarly, the intent behind an act of war can vary across acting in self-defence, securing resources, gaining profit or exerting political influence. The political context will therefore serve to both set out the overall nature of the violence as well as the foundation for determining whether it is justified or not. But in order to understand the different levels involved and where it might exist on the spectrum, it is necessary to detail the severity of the violation, the temporal length and repetition of the impact, as well as who is impacting whom.

Severity

The term 'severity' refers to the level of harm or damage caused as determined by the degree to which the impact violates the interest(s) or target, how often it happens or the number of entities targeted, and plays a key role in determining where on the spectrum the action is positioned. This means recognizing that these (vital) interests are not binary, whole one minute and utterly destroyed the next, but exist to varying degrees. In terms of causing harm, for example, each of our vital interests can be impacted to different degrees: people can suffer various levels of physical and mental pain; autonomy can be circumvented to different degrees depending on the control exerted over someone; their physical liberty restrained for different periods of time; and their privacy can be perceived as consisting of different levels where the more personal or intimate the information, the greater the expectation of privacy and the greater the harm caused when violated (von Hirsch, 2000; Marx, 2004). Importantly, examining the severity gives context to the different ways in which various interests can be violated. While some interests – physical and mental integrity, for example – will often be considered more important and therefore violations more violent, it is still dependent on the severity of the attack. For example, a prick on the finger is not considered more harmful than being incarcerated just because it is a physical violation as compared to a violation of liberty, meaning that the severity of the violation helps understand the specific level of harm caused. In terms of causing damage, often it can be measured in more quantifiable means. For example, loss of reputation, damage to property and loss of earnings can all be detailed in monetary value. Therefore, the level of damage caused can vary and can be understood in terms of its degree of impact and the associated physical, financial, reputational, institutional, accountable, integral and inconvenience costs.

The severity also includes the number of repetitions suffered or the temporal quality. That is, how often it happens and for how long. Baber points out that, 'intuitively, duration of a harmed state figures importantly in assessments of its seriousness ... being locked in the bathroom for 20 minutes is not a great harm, whereas being imprisoned for 20 years makes an important difference to a person's other interests' (Baber, 1987: 131). Over time, for example, what could be considered a low or trivial violation of our interests can become a more severe violation. Finally, the severity level depends on how many individuals are affected by the actions involved as well as any specific vulnerabilities of the target. By increasing the number of people who are violated, then the total combined violations of all those affected both directly and indirectly need to be included. There is also a compound effect here, where when many people are impacted the overall harm is far greater than the simple sum of their individual harms. In this way it is possible to think of how it might be possible to harm a 'society' or specific section of society. By targeting more than one person, or even targeting one person who typifies or represents a group, it is possible for it to harm a group; therefore the combined harm both on the individuals and what group of individuals represent must be taken into account.

Who on whom

Finally, which actors or entities are involved and their inter-relationship can play an important role in understanding and detailing the sort of violence involved, as well as playing an important role in defining the political nature. That is, whether it involves states, individuals, peoples, social groups or structures, as either the giver or the receiver of the violent action, the political nature can vary. Often the main actors involved include the state and its representatives and institutions, individuals, peoples and social groups (broadly categorized as 'non-state actors'), and structures. Each of these can then combine in a variety of relationships that often determines much of the taxonomy used. Most notably, state-on-state activities can include acts of armed conflict and war in its many different forms. While state-on-individuals/peoples political violence can range from its use of the criminal-judicial system to punish through capital punishment or imprisonment, to acts of police brutality, segregation, marginalization, victimization, counter-insurgency, torture and genocide. Violence between non-state actors can include ethnic conflict, as acts of violence are used between groups, though this can be sponsored or supported by state actors. While non-state-on-state political violence can consist of attacks against the state and its institutions, ranging from terrorism, insurgency, violent protest, rebellion, revolt, rioting, revolution and civil war, to acts of resistance which have the individual acting according to their own schema in contradiction to that of some other power (Gregg, 1993: 25; Profitt, 1996). Finally, structural violence refers to the harm that social and non-material structures cause people by preventing them from realizing their vital interests and basic needs, or even their secondary interests by restricting, distorting or prioritizing others.

For political hacking, the relationships involve multiple actors, including the hacker and its target and who that target is in turn targeting. In terms of the hackers, while they can vary from individuals to highly organized and defined groups with a set membership, or to large fluid collectives whose organization, structure, mandate and membership can fluctuate, they are essentially non-state actors. Whereas who they target can vary from cyber-systems to state actors, individuals, corporations, non-state organizations and non-state actors, crossing between and impacting both the cyber and real world. In turn, each of these targets can then be a threat to other political actors representing state-on-people violence, corporation-on-people violence or structural violence. These inter-actor relationships do not, in and of themselves, necessarily alter the level of the political violence on the spectrum, but they do give a framing that helps us better understand the type of political violence involved and the broader social, political and, importantly, ethical concerns.

Political hacking as political violence

As previously mentioned, 'political hacking' is distinguishable from hacks for personal profit – such as theft, fraud or blackmail – or hacks to test systems or to create chaos for its own sake. Even as a sub-field of hacking, however, political hacking still covers an extensive range of different aims, methods, impacts and justifications. It was also noted that there is a significant focus and use of 'hacktivism', which frames hacking as activism, and whose purpose is 'to highlight political or social causes' through non-violent means in response to a social issue (O'Malley, 2013: 140). This, however, ignores or marginalizes those aspects of contemporary political hacking that are more than disseminating a political message, but actively rely on the use of coercion, threats, destruction and force as a means of directly influencing or enabling change. The result is that those evaluative frameworks associated with hacktivism cannot accommodate the ethical use of violence. Hacktivism's association with political activism provides civil disobedience as its evaluative framework, which does offer an established avenue for arguing in support of some political hacking by making references to it as an established and recognized form of non-violent political participation. The problem with this is that civil disobedience 'does not condone violent or destructive acts against its enemies, focusing instead on nonviolent means to expose wrongs, raise awareness, and prohibit the implementation of perceived unethical laws by individuals, organizations, corporations or governments (Manion and Goodrum, 2000: 14). It is the 'principled and deliberate breach of law intended to protest unjust laws, politics, institutions, or practices and undertaken by agents broadly committed to basic norms of civility' (Delmas, 2018: 17); or the conscientious and communicative breach of law designed to demonstrate condemnation so as to direct a change in law, through non-violent means with a willingness to accept the consequences (Brownlee, 2012: 18). In all of these definitions non-violence sits at the centre of civil disobedience.

The contemporary hacks examined in this book, however, go beyond this conceptualization of hacktivism, arguing that many acts of political hacking necessarily use and rely on violence to further their political ends. For example, political hacking can include actions in the form of DDoS attacks, email bombs, virtual sit-ins, doxxing, leaks, viruses and malware, all of which are powerful because of the (threat of) coercive power or damage they cause. For instance, a 'virtual blockade is the virtual version of a physical sit-in or blockade: political activists visit a website and attempt to generate so much traffic towards the site that other users cannot reach it' (Wiemann, 2004: 4). The aim is to disrupt normal operations and prevent the target from using its facilities (Denning, 1999: 6). This is similar to one of the more infamous hacking tools known as a denial of service attack (DoS attack) where 'the party initiating the attack saturates the computer server hosting the target website with requests for information, dramatically increasing the consumption of computational resources and eventually causing the server to slow down or reset (Hampson, 2012: 518). While a distributed-denial of services (DDoS) attack is similar, it uses a network of multiple attacking computers: 'the initiating party activates a network of computers under its control, called a botnet, to multiply the power of the attack' (Hampson, 2012: 519). Voluntary DDoS attacks use computers which have ceded their control to the botnet computer or directly participate in the coordinated attack, whereas an involuntary DDoS involves individuals who take control of another's computer – referred to as a slave or zombie – to carry out the attack (O'Malley, 2013: 142). Similar tactics include the use of 'email-bombs', which involves bombarding a target with thousands of messages at once, effectively completely jamming a recipient's email inbox and making it impossible for legitimate emails to get through (Denning, 1999: 7). Website defacements involve hackers gaining access to a website and posting unauthorized messages, text, images or graphics on the site (O'Malley, 2013: 142). For example, a group of Portuguese hackers modified the websites of forty Indonesian servers in September 1998 to display the message 'Free East Timor' and included links to websites describing Indonesian human rights abuses (Harmon, 1999). Or when, in 1998, Milw0rm hacked the Indian Bhabha Atomic Research Centre so that its pages displayed a mushroom cloud with the text stating that 'If a nuclear war starts, you will be the first to scream' (Glave, 1998). Or, in another notable example, when Anonymous 'hacked the websites and posted messages protesting the Chinese government's strict censorship and control of its citizens' (BBC News, 2012).

Another tactic is to use 'doxxing', which is the act of revealing information online by 'dropping documents' that belong to someone else, and who has not given permission for them to be revealed. This can include revealing identifying or personal information belonging to an individual, such as their physical appearance, real name, home address, workplace, phone, financial and other personal information, or it can also include releasing an organization's privately owned information, such as databases on their clients, emails, technological developments and contracts. Gaining access to this information can consist of finding a weakness in the target's system, such as weak passwords or technical exploits, and then using that access to collect and distribute the information.

In some cases the damage could only be temporary; the servers hosting the information are not materially or physically damaged and following the attack often normal service can resume. But cyberspace and the Internet are much more than their physical servers, and are more about how people are allowed to interact with each other and the information shared and stored on there. Indeed, preventing access to a site can therefore represent reputational, financial, informational and social costs as well as harm to people if they are prevented from being able to pursue their own informational ends, something essential for maintaining and fulfilling their autonomy and privacy (often the central argument made by the hackers themselves). As a German court ruled, even the passive 'chaining oneself to a railing or an entrance gate or sitting in someone's way was equal to violence', given that it restricts liberty and autonomy (Celikates,

2016). Doxxing to release private information about an individual or organization therefore represents a violation of the target's privacy, and potentially a loss of reputation and income, and leaking documents, such as the unsanctioned release of confidential information (whether state or corporate) to news media outlets, can cause both direct damage or harm when the leak results in a backlash being visited upon those involved or subsequent harms related to how others use the information. And the use of viruses and malware often has a direct aim of causing physical damage to a network or system.

This runs counter to those who argue that real-world protesting can be simply transferred to cyberspace with the same conceptual understanding and justification. That is, while 'protesting on one's blog is akin to shouting from one's living room', there is no 'online equivalent to protesting outside a company's storefront or headquarters' (Delmas, 2018a: 66). The 'front' of a website is not the same as the front of a shop, facility or organization. Justified sit-ins were acts of civil disobedience during the civil rights movement because they were non-violent, provided a spectacle, highlighted a key point of discrimination and helped spread the news, and even though they did involve trespass the acts were performative and the performance did not seek to cause damage or harm but rather highlight the message. In the physical world, actions such as picketing, sit-ins and occupation movements are tolerated (to a varying degree) and limited to instances where people's lives are not being damaged or violated, and often the space being occupied is a 'public' one with traditional demarcations for the right to speech, association and expression for the protesters, and where the protest directly highlighted the inequality experienced. Protesters may hamper the ability to enter a location and demonstrators may hinder the ability to travel through the city normally, but they use the public space to their advantage. Cyberspace is different and such public spaces do not exist in the same way. Whether the website is privately owned or even a government-owned facility, legal test cases have determined that free speech protections like those outlined in the US First Amendment do not include using a website against the owners' wishes (Li, 2013: 313–15). Traditional public forums, such as streets or parks, do not buttress a publicly facing website to provide a space for protest. The result is that actions such as virtual-sit-ins, DDoS attacks, email bombs and website defacements are distinct from their real-world counterparts. They necessarily involve material damage to the owners through the loss of legitimate activity, even if it is only temporarily. For example, website defacement not only portrays a message similar to real-world graffiti, but it also actually undoes the purpose of the website, damaging it in an impactful way when people cannot access the information or service that they require, something clearly different to pasting a message on a building. Equally, physical sit-ins in an institution's foyer are truly an inconvenience, but as the

Wall Street protests showed, they do not physically prevent their operation. DDoS attacks, however, can shut down the mechanisms needed for the network's operation and interaction with other individuals.

At the other end of the spectrum, resorting to labelling political hacking as 'cyber-terrorism' is also unhelpful as it overestimates the level of violence and destruction used as well as the ultimate political agenda of the hack. Cyber-terrorism is 'the use of computer network tools to shut down critical national infrastructure (such an energy, transportation, government operations) or to coerce or intimidate a government or civilian population' (Lewis, 2002). Grouping cyber-terrorism with political hacking, even that which is destructive, fails to recognize that hacking's purpose is not to foster fear in a third party, nor is it aiming to cause widespread destruction like that seen in terrorism, but rather that those targeted are the intended audience of the attack and agents against whom the hackers are seeking to effect change (Lewis, 2002).

What this means, therefore, is that this often used and simplified division between hacktivism and cyber-terrorism ignores those hacks that necessarily or inherently use some form of political violence to achieve their ends, falling outside the realm of activist-based hacktivism, but are still arguably distinct from terrorism lacking the same magnitude of destruction and the aim of creating fear within a third-party audience (Jackson et al, 2011; Jackson and Pisoiu, 2018). This pushes political hacking into either of these camps, where it is either automatically rejected for its violent status as it falls under the activist framework or is hyper-securitized under the label of cyber-terrorism with treatment and punishments in far excess of what is actually carried out and an inability to see the benefit it could bring to society. Therefore, it is vital to understand both that political hacking does include a degree of violence as part of its activity, but that this can be justified when it meets the criteria outlined in the following chapter.

Conclusion

The purpose is not to offer any justification for the different acts or instances of political hacking at this stage, but rather to outline the way in which political violence can vary, shaping how political hacking can be understood, and that by creating a spectrum of political violence it is possible to recognize that hacking involves a broader range of activities than the existing definitions allow for while also giving nuance and detail to the different instances and forms of hacks. Creating this spectrum of political violence involves detailing the complex relationship between the nature of the damage or harm caused; the severity of that damage or harm; who is impacting whom; and the intent or political context of the impact. The metaphor of the spectrum allows for hacker activities to be placed on a graduated ladder so that in the next chapter a corresponding spectrum of justification can be created that offers different types or levels of justifications which can be separated out and then placed on a graded spectrum alongside the levels of harm or destruction. By doing this it is possible to portray the idea that there is a correlation between the two, and that in order to justify specific harms you must have the same or higher level of just circumstances present. The harm caused should be correlated to the justifying principles. As one goes up, so should the other.

2

An Ethical Framework for Hacking Operations

Introduction

Large, politically orientated hacker collectives such as Anonymous have targeted a range of actors over a diverse set of issues, all without a consistent set of ethical principles to guide or evaluate their activity. As previously noted, the challenge is that these actions by hackers necessarily use harmful or damaging actions on people or systems as a direct means of furthering their political goals, outside official systems sanctioned by the political community. But this does not inherently dismiss their actions as unjustified. Rather, it will be argued here that such actions can be justified when used to protect people from harm as a form of self-defence. To make this argument, this chapter will create an ethical framework based on the argument that people have a core set of vital interests that need to be protected, including maintaining one's physical and psychological integrity, autonomy, liberty and privacy. This need for protection creates a right to self-defence, including the right to defend others when they are threatened;, and when there are no other actors – whether it is due to a lack of ability, political will or because the state is the source of the threat – there to offer that protection then political hackers can fill the void. It will also argue that the right to be defended from harm is more important than waiting for state actors to offer the protection, and so just because hackers are outside the state does not automatically discount them as ethical actors. Another part of this ethical framework is the argument that both the political violence used by the political hackers and the self-defence justification expressed can exist to varying degrees. That is, the greater the level of damage caused by the political hack, the greater the threat it is countering needs to be to make it justified. As a result, this ethical framework will then form the basis of

---

Parts of this chapter have been initially examined in Bellaby, 2021.

the ethical debates in future chapters and give guidance on how society should react to these political hackers. To achieve this, it is first necessary to highlight the potential ethical role of the hacker; second, is to outline the essential criteria that need to be fulfilled for the act of political hacking to be justified, detailing what actions are justified towards what end; and third, to offer mechanisms that can aid in reaching these ethically justified decisions. The framework can therefore be used to both justify and condemn hacking depending on the circumstances, allowing an evaluation of political hacking both past and present.

Filling the void: hackers using political violence

One of the key criticisms levied at hacker activity is that they are private actors carrying out their own political ends through the use of political violence. So, while collectives such as Anonymous have engaged in what can broadly be referred to as digital resistance (Delmas, 2018a), digital disobedience (Scheuerman, 2016) or digital activism (Sauter, 2015), and use methods which range across the activist spectrum, a distinguishing feature of the type of political hacking examined here is the purposeful use of political violence. Indeed, these hacks necessarily use (the threat of) coercive violence to further their political ends.[1] This can include: distributed denial of service (DDoS) attacks where the normal traffic of a targeted server, service or network is disrupted by overwhelming it or the surrounding infrastructure with a flood of Internet traffic with the aim of either temporarily or permanently shutting it down, causing damage to both the target's infrastructure as well as their ability to interact with their clients and those clients' ability to pursue their own ends (Citron, 2014; Coleman, 2014: 3; Sauter, 2015; Douglas, 2016); 'doxxing', whereby private information about an individual or organization is collected and widely released online, causing harm through the violation of people's privacy, and potential loss of reputation and income (Citron, 2014; Douglas, 2016); and the release of confidential, often national security, information (whether state or corporate) to news media outlets, which can cause both direct damage through the leak, or subsequent harm depending on how others use the information (Leigh and Harding, 2011). Finally, hackers can use viruses and malware to cause damage to a network system (Denning, 1999: 1).

---

[1] This distinguishes it from hacktivism, which is a form of non-harmful digital activism, as well as cyber-terrorism which relies on 'the hack to cause grave harm ... such as loss of life, or severe economic damage', where the intent is cause fear to send a message to a third-party audience (Delmas, 2018a; see also Denning, 1999; Manion and Goodrum, 2000: 14; Himma, 2008: 200; Mansfield-Devine, 2011b; Hampson, 2012; O'Malley, 2013; Goode, 2015; Karagiannopoulos, 2018). For more on the distinction that separates out cyber-terrorism see Jordan and Taylor, 2004; Holt et al, 2017; Tanczer, 2017; Jackson and Pisoiu, 2018).

Given this necessary use of political violence, the first question, therefore, is whether hackers possess the necessary moral authority to use violence for a political objective when they act outside of the system. This is often contrasted against the normative authority states claim – a claim often made through their representation of the political body or protector of the polis. Indeed, there are strong arguments that the state is the only actor who can legitimately use political violence (Duff, 2011: 6). This includes the argument that there is a broad social contract where individuals give up their absolute rights to carry out their own private wars or pursuit of personal justice in return for the comfort and protection provided by the state.[2] The state therefore has the duty to ensure that individuals are protected, that rules are maintained, and that differences are arbitrated. In return there is a *prima facie* obligation to obey the rules and mechanisms established (Markel, 2011: 54). Hackers do not have any of this, and, moreover, when they carry out harmful activities, they in turn break the agreement not to carry out private acts of violence, and mark themselves as a threat to the social whole and the good found in the stability of the rule of law.

However, this does not necessarily reject hacking completely. The state's legitimate authority is not derived from its de facto position or its coercive sovereignty, but from its role as representative and protector of the political community (Norman, 1995: 118). States have value because of the role they play in an individual's life as the moral unit of concern: the moral authority or legitimacy of the state is based on its role in protecting vital interests and fundamental human rights (Fabre, 2008: 964). So, while there can be arguments in favour of the general obligation to obey authority when the state is furthering the protection of this moral unit, if the state is absent in its application of this role then others can, and should, act. If the state fails to uphold its end of the bargain, due to lack of will, capability, negligence, or because itself represents an unjustified source of harm, then it loses its legitimate authority in this specific instance. This supports those works, therefore, that seek to problematize the state as the sole legitimate authority that can use political violence in the international system, especially those looking to expand the concept of authority in the just war tradition (see Heinze and Steel, 2009). As Amy Eckert argues, 'The legitimate authority principle has become reduced to the issue of state authority. In its current formulation, the state has the sole authority

---

2 For classical social contract theory, including Thomas Hobbes and John Locke and modern political theories of the evolution of governance like that of Robert Nozick, civil government springs forth from the *state of nature*, a pre-social anarchic state in which individual action is at its peak (Nozick, 1974; Hobbes, 1985 [1651]; Locke, 1988 [1689]).

to wage war, and because non-state actors, by their very definition, cannot satisfy this principle, their use of force is inherently unethical' (Eckert, 2020: 84; see also Williams, 2008; Parry, 2017). However, if the underlying value of the state is the political community rather than the state per se, this reshapes how legitimate authority can, and should, be located. In practice, though, the use of violence and the provision of security has already been diversified away from the state (both willingly and unwillingly), challenging its monopoly on the legitimate use of force (Singer, 2003; Avant, 2005; Eckert, 2020).

As a result, arguments can be made that rather than fighting against the political community and even the state, private actions such as those carried out by political hackers can reinforce the importance of social norms and that they are replicating the important protective role the state should play for the political community: that they can 'claim to respect the law even more than the sitting government officials, since [they take] it seriously enough to want to see it enforced' (Dumsday, 2009: 59). Les Johnson argues that through organized and coordinated forms of political violence, non-state actors can be justified when they act as the state should be acting: for example, when the state has good laws that are misapplied or not being enforced; when the state has failed to enact good laws; or when unjust laws are being enforced (Johnston, 1996; Reynolds, 2015). Such activities, while outside the normal state-sanctioned infrastructure, are instances where private actors represent what the state should be doing or where they seek to circumvent the harm the state is causing. When the hacker, for example, provides people with technology that allows access to the Internet when it is blocked by their government, or raises awareness about or seeks to directly stop a particular political agenda that actively harms or discriminates part of society, they are not denouncing key ethical and social norms but are emphasizing them, while highlighting the failure of the state or marking it as the source of the wrong. These hackers seek to maintain those ethical and social norms that are already in existence, that are widely already agreed upon and have already moral authority. Developing an ethical framework for hacking, therefore, rests on the core argument that this activity is about replicating that good the state represents in people's lives by acting to protect people as the state should, albeit outside the usual mechanisms.

Therefore, in instances where good laws are not being enforced then the laws themselves can act to provide both legitimacy and guidance to the hacker. Such laws already represent a source of good in society, are agreed upon by the political community and are recognized as being worthwhile. In this instance the hacker can appeal to the law as it stands, and in doing so acts as the state should. This allows a more nuanced and detailed set of instances for the hacker to act, given the established body of law. But in cases where the state is enforcing 'laws that are actually evil or unjust and, as such, do not afford protection to members of society that they should' (Reynolds, 2015: 441), reference should be made to the more fundamental interests individuals possess (which are detailed more fully later), including their vital interests in maintaining their physical or mental integrity, autonomy, liberty or privacy. For example, as a justification for acts against established authorities (such as the state and its established rule of law), Carl Cohen argues that specific laws can be deemed as invalid if they deprive someone from constitutionally guaranteed rights (Cohen, 1970); while David Lefkowitz refers to the need for a clear 'undefeated moral reason' when acting against the state (Lefkowitz, 2007: 206); and for Rawls, that the laws must be clear 'principles for assigning and servicing fundamental rights and liberties' to have authority (Rawls, 2009: 245). Recognizing such transgressions, as well as what counts as a good law, can be aided by appealing to universal statutes, the Universal Declaration of Human Rights for example, as they offer a codified version of our vital human interests and can act as a source of international authority from which the hackers can draw. However, due to the various localized interpretations of such norms they can only act to provide a thin layer of protection, a minimum level to which all people's vital interests should be ensured. For example, people should, *other things being equal*, be free from pain and mental anguish, should have spaces where they know and can reasonably expect to be in private and have control over their information, be allowed freedom of space, and have the capacity to decide for themselves how to make decisions, including being aware and in possession of relevant information necessary to aid in their decision-making processes.

Significantly, in making this calculation the initial position should be that legitimate authority rests with the state, and only when it fails to fulfil its ethical obligation can other actors intervene. This means recognizing that, on the one hand, no state is perfect and such imperfections do not make the whole state a failure and undermine all its legitimate laws and activities. While on the other hand, even near-just states can fail in specific areas and thus create a space for intervention. This means distinctions are needed between instances where the state fails because it is not infallible in an uncertain world and those where the state has acted negligently. In the former case, if the processes are generally sound and are not in themselves problematic, then the failure or the occasional miscarriage of justice is not sufficient to argue that the state has failed in its attempt to offer protection. Failure is different to negligence, whereby the latter denotes deficiency in exercising appropriate care and judgment – whether wilful or not – that results in the harm of another. This can include intended and unintended negligence where the actor fails to maintain the general ethical expectations of society as well as the specific additional standards of their profession.[3] For example, systematic discrimination such as racism or homophobia, corruption or failure of the duty of care are instances of negligence, while plea-bargaining, unforeseen accidents, or rules that in the majority of cases provide just results but do fail (and whose failure could not have been anticipated) represent mistakes in an otherwise just system. Therefore, the hack can only be justified in those instances where the state has neglectfully failed, recognizing that in near-liberal states such instances can occur due to negligence, incompetence, inability or lack of will. It is just that in authoritarian states such failures are more likely to be widespread, systematic and of a greater magnitude.

This can include, for example, when the state is the source of the threat. For instance, *en masse* violations of vital interests such as freedoms of speech, privacy or association mean the state loses its legitimate authority and the hackers can intervene. Or second, when the state is unwilling or unable to prevent harm because it does not have the technical ability or manpower, though hackers should relinquish authority once the ordinary mechanisms are sufficiently available. For example, dark web activity entails a significant degree of technical skills and time, but once information about the harmful activity has been collected it should be forwarded for state authorities to act. Third, this also includes cases in which the state is unwilling to act to protect people – through a lack of political will, for example – despite clear and compelling evidence of a threat. Appealing to legal cannon on evidence and balance of probabilities can aid the hackers in knowing how and when to act. However, simply disagreeing with the state's legitimately arrived decision is not sufficient. If, for example, the court has reviewed a case, the correct processes were followed, and the judgment was one of not guilty, then, short of new evidence, the hackers should not act. Therefore, the aim is not to justify all forms of private political violence, but only in very specific instances where the state has negligently failed, and then only when there is a just end as detailed in the next section.

Justifying the act

The political justifications often directly stated by hackers can be quite varied, ranging from delivering punishment against wrongdoers, including paedophiles, hate groups and corrupt businesses, to protecting fundamental civil and human rights, such as the right to information, expression and

---

[3]   For example, 'professional negligence' demands that individuals within a profession or position of authority are held to a higher standard where they are charged with additional duties to protect those within their care and are expected to have higher than average abilities, knowledge or training and should act diligently and knowingly (Horsey, 1994: 974; Lepora and Goodin, 2013).

speech.[4] Or they can reflect a broad political orientation or ideology, ranging from generic left-leaning and socialist ideals, to anti-right-wing sentiments, to specific statements on anti-establishment or anti-corporativism, or to radical freedom of online information where information should be free for sharing regardless of the original owner of the information.[5] To this end, despite the different objectives put forward by hackers it will be argued that acting in self-defence/defence of others can offer a way of understanding if and when the hack is justified. Moreover, by examining the hack in terms of self-defence, it is possible to see further how private individuals can act to use political violence as legitimate agents.

In terms of self-defence, while there is significant debate regarding its underlying justifications, and Fiona Leverick offers a very strong review of consequentialist and person partiality approaches, it will be argued here that at its core the individual first and foremost has the right to protect their own life, even at the expense of another's; and that when an attacker represents a threat they forfeit their usual protections that prevent the victim from killing them (Alexander, 1976; Montague, 1989; Thomson, 1991; Otsuka, 1994; Kasachkoff, 1998; Leverick, 2006). The starting position here is that the right to life is considered a fundamental, if not the fundamental, human right. Moreover, this is a Hohfeldian claim-right, where the importance of the right to life is such that it places duties on other individuals to act so as not to violate that right (Hohfeld, 1913). There is a duty to respect the right to life. This duty means that it is not just the victim who has a right to act, but others can intervene to prevent the attack (Wasserman, 1987; Thomson, 1991: 306; Christopher, 1998). Cecile Fabre extensively discusses this point, arguing that the:

> victim's fundamental interest in surviving A's attack is not merely protected by a right to kill A; it is also protected by a prima facie power to transfer that right to a third party … to claim otherwise is to impose an arbitrary restriction on V's ability to promote this fundamental interest of hers. (Fabre, 2012: 63)

This created duty not only prevents violating an individual's right to life but also actively promotes others to avoid violating it and allows defenders to intervene when appropriate. Importantly, this means the individual's right to self-defence has primacy over other considerations, such as limiting the

---

[4] For example, Operation Tunisia and Operation Egypt sought to provide tools to circumvent state online censorship.

[5] For example, Operation Megaupload hacked United States Department of Justice, the United States Copyright Office, the Federal Bureau of Investigation, the MPAA, Warner Brothers Music, the RIAA and the HADOPI in retaliation for the shutting down of the file-sharing platform Megaupload.

legitimate use of political violence to only state representatives. That is, the victim or defender need not wait for a state representative – such as the police – to intervene before they can carry out their necessary protections. While practical considerations often promote turning to state representatives, the individual's fundamental right to defend themselves comes first.

While much of the self-defence literature, especially that which focuses on wartime killing, is often interested in protecting life and limb and the right to use deadly force to defend oneself as a result, this can be expanded to recognize the other key aspects of the human condition that need protection. That is, protecting oneself should include protecting all our vital interests: those preconditions that all individuals have, by virtue of the human condition, that need to be fulfilled if they are to continue living their own version of the good life. These vital interests include, probably most obviously, the interest in maintaining one's physical integrity and the need to be free from pain. But this should be expanded to also include psychological integrity, autonomy, liberty and privacy. These vital interests are needed to be maintained for the individual to be able to flourish, and if they are violated or fall below a minimum level, then the individual is harmed. By understanding how people are harmed in terms of their vital interests in this way, it is possible to highlight the threats that they can face from various actors – including the state, its representatives or its laws – as well as the harm or damage that can be produced by the hackers. This allows for a greater understanding of the harmful actions carried out by both the threatening agent and the hackers in their act of defence of others.

Expanding vital interests in cyberspace

Of these vital interests, physical and psychological integrity should be the most self-explanatory. Maintaining the integrity of the physical body is one of the most fundamental interests an individual has. The body is the physical home and representation of the *self*. The body represents the primary mechanism through which an individual experiences the world and carries out his wishes. If the body is damaged it severely hinders the ability to actualize any other aspect of the human experience. As such, there is a clear interest in protecting the body, both as the physical home of the *self* and the primary means through which an individual can actualize and interact with the rest of reality. If the physical body is damaged or violated to the extent that its integrity falls below a threshold level, it becomes unable to function correctly.[6] While not intrusively an issue for hackers given the

---

[6]   This includes the experience of pain, which is a harmful state to exist in and when the individual is suffering from physical pain he is unable to conceive of pretty much

metaphysical nature of cyberspace, given the reliance on the Internet hackers can use their online power to influence policy, practices and activities that are harming people physically.

If the body is the physical representation or the 'home' of the self and the means through which an individual experiences and actualizes the world, then the 'psyche' is the individual's metaphysical home and the *place* where the world is experienced and actualized. The psyche is responsible for one's faculty of reason or the sum of a person's intellectual capabilities, representing the immaterial and actuating part of one's life. Feinberg notes that there must exist a 'minimal intellectual acuity, emotional stability, absence of groundless anxieties' if the individual is to continue with his more ultimate interests (Feinberg, 1984: 37). To damage an individual's psyche is to prevent him from experiencing, actualizing and interacting with the world as he usually would. As Martha Nussbaum argues, if an individual's mentality or psyche is severely damaged then 'we may judge ... that the person is not really a human being at all' (Nussbaum, 2000: 73).

Beyond these quite clear vital interests, protecting the human condition should also include ensuring for people's vital interest in autonomy, liberty and privacy. Autonomy is the capacity for self-rule; to decide for oneself, without external manipulation or interference, what shape one's own life will take. This involves 'being able to form a conception of the good and to engage in critical reflection about the planning of one's life – the protection of the liberty of conscience' (Nussbaum, 2000: 79). Maintaining the integrity of an individual's autonomy requires, first, that the individual's ability to function rationally is protected, including the capacity to make decisions freely, without undue influence, control or distortion. The autonomous agent must be able to act for 'reasons all the way down according to their actions and according to their reasons' (Herman, 1996: 228). This means that any form of lying, manipulation, coercion or distorting influences violates an individual's autonomy (Monroe and Malle, 2014). It also prioritizes access to relevant knowledge so that the individual has the capacity to plan, choose and reflect on options in terms of arguments, evidence and potential choices so as to make a decision (Frankfurt, 1971: 7). People need access to the necessary information to make specific decisions, as well as access to wider sources of information to develop their overall decision-making capacity. This means that people, *all other things being equal*, should not be lied to as their decisions are forced to be made on the reality the lie creates, and that

---

anything else. When the body is in extreme pain it is completely debilitated, unable to conceive of anything else as it 'forcibly severs our concentration on anything outside of us; it collapses our horizon to our own body and the damage we feel in it ... the world of man or woman in great pain is a world without relationships or engagements, a world without exterior' (Luban, 2005: 1430).

they should have access to information to be able to critically reflect on their options. Lack of relevant information can violate an individual's autonomy as they are unable to decide how to make decisions regarding the world around them and those they interact with, and are unable to decide how they should (re)act. Furthermore, they must be free from undue coercion or influence to ensure that their decisions are based on their own set of rationales. This includes being free from both explicit coercion as well as implicit coercion such as the cyber-panoptic gaze, where individuals act differently if they think they are being watched, conforming to the standards of what they believe is expected of them by their watchers. Indeed, given cyber-surveillance's ability to transcend space and time limitations and bring the asymmetric gaze of the panopticon to non-institutionalized spaces, it can detrimentally affect an individual's autonomy as they start to 'self-discipline' their actions and surrender to the wishes of the observers as the individual 'becomes the principle of his own subjection' (Foucault, 1979: 202–3; see also Lyon, 1994: 65; McCahill, 1998). This interest in autonomy creates several rights that are of specific importance to hackers and cyberspace, including, but not limited to, the right to free speech and expression, the right to know, to share information and to be informed, the need for oversight and transparency, and the right to associate as people wish (Brison, 1998a: 312). For online activity, this places protections around accessing and sharing information, using cyberspace as a place and means for associating with others, and protecting against surveillance of online activity.

Closely connected to autonomy is the interest an individual has in liberty. As John Stuart Mill notes, Liberty is 'not the so-called Liberty of the Will ... but Civil, or Social Liberty: the nature and limits of the power which can be exercised by society over the individual' (Mill, 1991: 5).[7] If autonomy is the freedom *to* decide one's will, then liberty is the freedom *from* constraints on acting out that will. As such, liberty is often simply defined as the 'absence of interference or control' (Feinberg, 1973: 7), whereby defending an individual's liberty is to limit the extent of intervention by other individuals or society. For example, if others prevent an individual from doing what they could otherwise do, they are, to that degree, 'unfree'.[8] This means that the individual is afforded the right to be free from outside forces that wish to

---

[7]   For more on the distinction between 'social freedom' (liberty) and 'freedom of will' (autonomy) see Isaiah Berlin who points out that the question 'who governs me?' is logically distinct from the question of 'how far does government interfere with me?' (Berlin, 1969: 130).

[8]   Violation of liberty implies the *deliberate interference* with one's activities. Berlin notes how Helvetius made this point very clearly: 'the free man is the man who is not in irons, nor imprisoned in a gaol ... it is not lack of freedom not to fly like an eagle or swim like a whale' (Berlin, 1969: 122).

control, alter or interfere with the actualization of his plans.[9] For example, external constraints might include physical barriers or coercive threats since, as Joseph Raz argues, acts of coercion directly encroach upon the freedom to act by eliminating options or courses of action otherwise available to an agent (Raz, 1986: 369, 154). This interest in liberty can play an essential part in the right to association as the individual should be free to convene, including in cyberspace, with those they wish unless it represents a more significant harm.

Finally, privacy is another vital interest that has become fundamental to how the online space is used and discussed, though as a political concept it is often challenging to create a single definition.[10] Indeed, the 'umbrella' of the privacy concept can include a range of prohibitions and claims, from privacy as a psychological state (Weinstein, 1971: 94), to others defining privacy as the extent to which 'information about them is communicated to others' (Westin, 1967: 7; see also Breckenridge, 1970: 1; Altman, 1976: 7; Reiman, 1976: 42; for 'selective disclosure' see Fried, 1968: 475; Miller, 1971: 25; Laufer and Wolfe, 1977: 34), while some see it purely as a physical state of affairs, being separated off from the rest of society (Brandeis and Warren, 1980).[11] This can mean that privacy is used to protect, among other things, authorship, control over one's body, solitude in one's home, and control over information about one's self (Benn, 1971: 3). By threading these various conceptualizations together, we can outline privacy as both an issue of *boundaries* and as *control*. By conceptualizing privacy as a *boundary* this reflects the many established spaces throughout society that mark out areas where outside intrusion is unwelcome. These boundaries separate out what is private on the inside from that which is public on the outside. Over-stepping the mark, as it were, and violating an established boundary means violating that person's privacy. This protects intrusions upon oneself, one's family, home, relationships and communications with others. These boundaries can be physical – walls, clothes or bags, for example – or metaphysical, like 'personal space'. Privacy as *control*, however, is the right of the individual to control those things pertaining to themselves, that is, 'the control we have over information about ourselves' (Fried, 1968: 475) or the 'control over

---

[9]   The term 'plan' is here intended to refer merely to whatever it is that a person broadly wants to do in and with his life.

[10]   Arthur Miller declared that privacy is 'difficult to define because it is exasperatingly vague and evanescent' (Miller, 1971: 25), and Julie Innes states that the legal and philosophical discourse on privacy is in a 'state of chaos' (Innes, 1996: 3), while William Beaney has noted that 'even the most strenuous advocate of a right to privacy must confess that there are serious problems in defining the essence and scope of this right' (Beaney, 1966: 253).

[11]   Theorists who define privacy as 'to be let alone' see Konvitz, 1966: 279; Freund, 1971; Beytagh, 1975: 455; Monagham, 1977: 414; Bloustein, 1978: 123.

one's personal affairs' (Gross, 1971: 169). Privacy conceived as thus can often equate to the notion of property rights. Judith Thomson argues that, while 'we have fairly stringent rights over our property, we have very much more stringent rights over our own persons' (Thomson, 1975: 303). The individual's body is theirs intrinsically, inherently theirs without question. This claim includes the self and any extensions of that self, and, importantly, to authorship. Someone's image, voice or even personal details work in the same way as any other property: an individual can sell the right to them or they may invite someone to use them, but if they decide that they no longer wish for others to use them then their property right is violated if another continues to do so. According to this notion of ownership, 'one's actions and their history 'belong' to the self which generated them and [are] to be shared only with those with whom one wishes to share them' (Shils, 1966: 290). Adam Carlyle Breckenridge argues that this means that 'privacy is the claim of the individual to determine the extent to which he wishes to share himself with others' (Breckenridge, 1970: 1), while the notion of the 'romantic author' gives the individual control over those things they create as they mix their unique personality with ideas, fixing them in some medium, and produce something that is automatically and intrinsically theirs (Boyle, 1997: 54). This can include artwork as well as a 'telephone conversation, personal diary, love letter, or email', all of which are owned by the individual by his creating them (Kang, 1998: 1207).

This conceptualization of privacy provides for online protections over what people do, whom they communicate with, what they communicate, and to be free from general observation. It also includes a right to anonymity. Anonymity creates a very specific boundary around oneself and issues stringent controls over one's identity. The zone of protection prevents people from accessing anything about them: the self is demarcated off from the rest of society and all information pertaining to the self is restricted, with selective release of authored information to the rest of the world (Schwartz, 1961). Moreover, in an increasingly surveilled world, especially from corporations and governments, anonymity acts as a protection and counters the growth and diversification of cyber-surveillance, data-mining and dataveillance. Anonymity can represent an important protection from retribution or revenge, especially for minorities who are afraid and other marginalized voices. As a result, it can encourage diversity of expression.

Vital interests and self-defence

All of these rights are of such importance that they cry out for protection, and create obligations on others not to infringe upon them. So, while self-defence is often examined in terms of maintaining one's physical integrity, it should also be understood as the right of the individual to protect their privacy, autonomy and liberty. Using the 'self-defence' terminology to refer to protecting one's non-physical vital interests might cause some to pause, but this is more because of the focus in the literature on discussions over when it is right to kill another to stop an impending aggressor, rather than there being any lack of there being a right to act to protect one's other vital interests from the unjustified infringement by others. For example, the privacy literature extensively discusses the different instances and types of defensive barriers one can erect and the actions one can take to stop others from accessing personal information – whether legal, physical or metaphorical.[12] Equally, the literature on autonomy argues for even forcible responses on those who wish to control one's ability to make and perform one's own informed decisions (Frankfurt, 1971; Feinberg, 1973; Lindley, 1986; Herman, 1996; Nussbaum, 2000). This conceptualization helps give greater credence to arguments where a victim could be justified in harming an attacker who threatens their non-physical vital interests, such as those who suffer psychological and emotional harm. For example, this stresses the uniquely horrific harms of rape as it adds the severe psychological, emotional and autonomy harms to the physical (Laugerud, 2021); or it could also give greater weight to victims of spousal abuse who suffer psychological torment, or are abused through controlling and manipulative behaviour; or even torture which relies on psychological and emotional attacks such as degradation, humiliation and fear. What is critical is that an individual's vital interests are fundamental to the human condition, require protection, place duties on others not to infringe on them unjustly, and in turn give the individual the right to defend through some appropriate and proportional action from others infringing on them. Importantly for this argument, understanding self-defence as more than just physical protection is important because it highlights other key, cyber-related interests that need protection – such as the interest in autonomy and its implications for the right to information.

Therefore, there is an important relationship between the vital interest being threatened and the justified appropriate means for achieving the necessary protection. A key part of this is understanding that these interests are not binary, whole one minute and destroyed the next, but occur and are impacted in different ways and to different extents, shaping different types of justified defensive activities. The type of self-defence justified, therefore, is determined by the particular vital interest threatened, the severity and duration of the threat, and its temporal proximity (Rescher, 1972: 5; Feinberg, 1984: 37). For example, each of our vital interests can

---

[12] For the right of privacy and the limits – whether as control or boundaries – see Westin, 1967; Fried, 1969; Thomson, 1975; Shils, 1996; Marx, 1998; Paine, 2000; Fairfield, 2005.

be impacted to different degrees: people can suffer various levels of physical and mental pain; their autonomy can be circumvented to different degrees; their physical liberty restrained for different periods of time; and their privacy can be perceived as consisting of different levels where the more personal or intimate the information the more significant the expectation of privacy and the greater the harm caused when violated (Feinberg, 1984: 46; von Hirsch, 2000; Marx, 2004: 234). Thus, for threats that are of a lesser magnitude than killing or severe pain, while there might not be a justification to kill in self-defence there could be justification for a low-level physical response, loss of property and resources, or sanctions (Pattison, 2018).

Furthermore, this more flexible conceptualization of self-defence has a key temporal aspect. Many self-defence justifications include a feeling of imminence, such as Thomson's innocent who is about to be run down by a truck, where the threat posed to the victim is very nearly upon them, which means the probability of the threat materializing is high and there are no opportunities for less harmful counterattacks (Thomson, 1991: 283). However, imminence is not always helpful when considering threats which are highly likely to occur but are far away; or where the threat is the systematic and widespread erosion of vital interests; or where the only viable form of defence is when the threatening actor themselves no longer represents an immediate threat – most notably in the case of women who kill their abusive husbands while they sleep. As a result, the self-defence literature distinguishes between 'self-defence against present definite threats … definite future threats … as well as indefinite potential threats' (Lee, 2018: 346; see also Walzer, 2000). These temporal and probability distinctions in turn shape the type of defensive action the potential victim can take. That is, while imminent threat to life is often used in justification of killing in self-defence, threats which are more temporarily distant can still be defended against through non-lethal, though still harmful, defensive actions such as restricting the liberty of the threat, reputational and financial harms, and temporary physical harm such as unconsciousness (Pattison, 2018).

In terms of hacking, therefore, what this means is that the hack used should reflect the threat posed. That is, in those instances where the individual's rights to information are being circumvented, then the defensive act that is justified is to provide individuals with greater online protection or the ability to circumvent state online censorship tools to protect their vital interest in privacy and autonomy.[13] In comparison, if the threat posed is

---

[13] The most famous of these is China's 'Golden Shield Project' – also known as the Great Firewall of China – that not only censors online content but also systematically probes for and shuts down any programs that might try to aid access to outside information. See TOR (2015).

to the individual's physical and mental integrity, then following the more traditional arguments of self-defence the hackers are justified in using more destructive means (though given the likelihood that an individual's life is not going to be in imminent danger then deadly force would not be justified), while in instances where the threat has more direct implications for an individual's ability to act as a free political agent, then the hack should be used to provide that agency, using proportional force to the degree to which the individual's autonomy is being controlled or subverted.

Wider consequences and protecting innocents

Additional limits are necessary in order to guide the hacker while also preventing unjustified harm in terms of level of attack and the targets impacted. One limit is proportionality, which raises two different requirements: first, there needs to be a threshold that must be reached before the hacker can act because not every small insult or injury warrants the type of damage caused. Second, the response itself must be proportional to the problem faced. With regard to the first point, hacking is essentially an extraordinary response, a situation where the normal mechanisms of the state and its institutions are deemed to have failed. The private action is supporting the ethical role of the state in its idealized form; it is not intended to replace the state per se. It should therefore seek not to be the norm. In an idealized situation it would not be needed. Therefore, it should limit itself only to those failings that are clear and significant. For example, 'rude behaviour in traffic even where there isn't an adequate police presence would not suffice to justify a vigilante response. Nor would rude behaviour on an Internet message board' (McReynolds, 2015: 427).

To make the second calculation on the overall benefit of the hack, key critical questions can be asked to help guide decision-making, including, first, what level of harm is caused by the hack? Most hacks will necessarily entail some form of damage. For example, this could range from financial costs where a website or network is rendered inoperable, or reputational costs as systems are undermined and/or embarrassing information is revealed, to costs to one's privacy or autonomy as private information is stolen and released, or to even costs to people's lives if critical infrastructures are shutdown or hindered. These damages must not exceed the perceived benefit of the hack, and in doing so this limits the hack from escalating. This means detailing what benefits the hack will provide as a positive in the calculation, such as providing increased access to online information and enabling freedom of expression, or preventing the violation of an individual's privacy or autonomy. Finally, what harms are allowed to continue if the hack is not carried out? For example, who is being harmed or is likely to be harmed and what is the extent of the harm if the status quo is allowed to continue? So, if an individual's right to information is being limited then the hack must correspond and correct this harm by giving them greater access; whereas if their physical security is threatened then this would represent a justification for a greater hacker attack that sought to prevent this harm from happening, such as coercing or even harming the threatening agent. There are, however, limits to the necessary calculations hackers have to make. For example, unforeseen and/or unintended consequences cannot be expected to be included in the moral calculation made by hackers. Similar to the doctrine of double effect, actions with foreseen damage can be permitted when the harm is not directly intended and the means to achieving the good have a proportionate end.

Finally, the attack must discriminate between legitimate and illegitimate targets. The underlying argument is that those individuals who make themselves a threat or do wrong essentially waive or forfeit the normal protections they have from being interfered with (Nagel, 1986: 162). It can be argued, therefore, that the harm directly inflicted through the hack should only negatively affect those who have either done wrong or who pose a threat. This can include not only individuals who have caused or will cause others harm, but organizations and states as well. In these latter cases the attacks can either be targeted against the offending systems or structures, or those individuals directly responsible for them and their continuation of the harm. Broadly speaking this would mean that the hack should only directly affect those who are the source of the problem and not impact 'innocent' bystanders. However, this can be quite flexible, with different hacks being justified against different actors depending on their role. In this way, involvement can be seen as a spectrum, where depending on one's role in the threat, the level of harm caused by the hack should vary. At one end are those (whether people or institutions) who have actively fostered a highly unethical state of affairs – including perpetuating or carrying out systematic physical attacks against others, for example – making them legitimate targets for harmful hacks, while at the other end there are those who are minimally complicit – by failing to act when they reasonably could have but who have not directly contributed, for example – making them only targets for hacks that minimally impact them, that is a mild irritation or inconvenience for instance.

Decision-making and limiting bias

At the core of this book is the argument that hackers can be legitimate when their activities are used to protect others from unjustified harm and when no other actors, traditionally the state, are able or willing to intervene. This places the right to defend others as primacy over making sure that more established actors are the ones to act. That is, one does not need to wait for the police before defending someone else's life. However, there are still some ethically important practical mechanisms used to help guide decision-making that, as much as possible, aim to achieve the best ethical end, so that the correct individual is subjected to the appropriate type and level of response. Indeed, traditional mechanisms such as due process, right to appeal, transparency, right to representation, and complaint mechanisms are valuable because they represent mechanisms for ensuring the best form of action; for trying to ensure the right action is carried out to the right individual, or that all individuals' rights are treated equally. The concern is that hackers could be prone to making biased, politically partisan or incorrect decisions.

So, while the ethical criteria can inform what an ethically justified hack might look like, additional decision-making mechanisms can play an important ethical role as they act to increase the likelihood of an appropriate decision being made while also reassuring the rest of the political community. Part of this is drawing out some of the key lessons from deliberative democracy concepts and institutions and the value they give both normatively and practically. This includes the value of having an engaged, critically reflective, open, inclusive and deliberative set of processes to increase the likelihood of reaching a better version of the truth sought while also limiting bias and unjustified political agendas (see Greenwalt, 1989). Indeed, Chambers argues that even in secretive environments, a deliberative ethos can still be replicated 'applying the publicity test by welcoming diversity of opinion' (Chambers, 2004: 408). This highlights the need for mechanisms that instil a process of engagement and dialogue; that there are mechanisms for discussion, interrogation and review. The devil, however, is often in the detail, and while it is not the aim here to give organizational specifics, underlying principles can be outlined so it is possible to foresee what useful tools might look like. This would include, firstly, a deliberation process to allow critique, debate and reflection to minimize the likelihood of personal bias. Hacker intentions, objectives and demands should allow for others to reflect on their reasoning. Second, a means for publicly debating these objectives and preferences can help ensure the logic is sufficiently interrogated. This could be supported by a means of collecting and sharing different opinions and giving individuals the opportunity to voice objections or provide new information. While these mechanisms do not guarantee an ethical decision will be made, they have value in increasing its likelihood, and by presenting the process publicly reassure the political community as to the deliberative process.

While there might be concerns that such mechanisms are not feasible due to hacker anonymity and given their decentralized and anti-hierarchical structure, this is not necessarily the case. In practice, being decentralized, anti-hierarchical and anti-leader does not necessarily mean that there are no decision-making processes or discussions in place, nor that they cannot be made more systematic and engaging. Philip Gray argues that having an anti-leader, non-hierarchical structure can facilitate discussion and action, allowing for greater flexibility, adaptability, broader appeal and inclusivity, while still being able to make decisions in a timely and directive manner (Gray, 2013). While these principles might initially seem counter to the idea of the lone hacker wreaking havoc from their private rooms, many hacker collectives exhibit such behaviours. Indeed, the Anonymous super-organism, whereby individuals coalesce around a particular cause and cooperate to produce the necessary results, operates in a similar methodology to the 'occupy movement' whereby individuals come together to fulfil a specific goal but move away again once the movement is over (Serracino-Inglott, 2013). This fluid and open structure necessarily invites dialogue and debate, albeit through non-traditional avenues. The internal decisions are already typified by horizontality and consensus, where a plurality of opinion and a reliance on mass contribution limits bias, and as Coleman details, through the 'public channels' Anonymous does debate and vote on operations (Coleman, 2014: 101–5). Indeed, the anti-leader ethos actively promotes discussion and voting procedures in order to enable a decision-making process. However, these processes should be encouraged through more explicit, public and open dialogue on online public forums with an established decision-making process. For example, there are already established platforms for sharing of ideas that rate ideas and have proven useful in generating a collective understanding of a topic from a diverse global membership. Most notable among these is reddit.com, a social news aggregation and content rating website that allows members to submit content – such as links, text posts and images – that is then voted up or down by other members.[14] Anonymity can still be maintained and it can reflect an anti-hierarchical ethos, though making it more officially open to outside involvement and formalized to ensure alternative points of view.

Overall, this framework does not discount individuals or smaller groups from acting, rather these inclusive mechanisms increase the likelihood of a more reflective decision being made and allows agents to be aware of the implications of their own shortcomings and decision-making.

Levels of justification and political violence

Making this evaluation by expanding the conceptualization of self-defence to include all of our vital interests, while also taking a more flexible understanding of the level of threat they can come under, and therefore the type of defensive act they justify, can allow for a more nuanced and

---

[14] See https://www.redditinc.com

flexible set of ethical criteria going forward. In the future chapters on applying these ethical criteria more detail will be given on which vital interest is threatened – whether physical, psychological, autonomy, liberty or privacy – along with how they relate to the political hacking operations examined. What was argued in Chapter 1 was that political hacking can cause varying levels of harm or damage depending on its negative impact, and that, as such, different activities could be spread along a spectrum of political violence. Equally, the justifying criteria can also be conceptualized as possessing different degrees in which they can exist and therefore can justify different forms of politically violent hacking. At its simplest, this is the argument that the greater the damage the hack is going to cause, the greater the threat, the gains, the more vital the interest, or the more people in need of protection there will need to be to make it justified.

Deploying the metaphor of the spectrum of justification is helpful because it illustrates how political hacking consists of various activities, each of which can cause a different degree of harm or damage in their activity, as outlined in Chapter 1. Similarly, the justification criteria argued for here can also exist to varying degrees depending on the context. It is therefore possible to portray the idea that there is a correlation between the two, and that in order to justify certain harms you must have the same or higher level of justifying political hacking criteria present.

This evaluation method requires detailing the extent to which both the hacker and the threatening agent they are fighting are damaging these vital interest(s) or causing wider damages. This includes recognizing that while some vital interests such as physical and mental integrity might appear to take precedence over the other interests, such as autonomy, liberty or privacy, this is not necessarily always the case and one's vital interests should be taken together as a complex matrix with all of them needing to be maintained. For example, a prick on the finger is not considered more harmful than being incarcerated just because it is a physical violation compared to a violation of liberty. Significantly, vital interests make a chain whereby the whole chain is no stronger than its weakest link (Rescher, 1972: 5; Feinberg, 1984: 37). An excess of one will not necessarily make up for the lack of another interest: offering an excess of physical security cannot be used as a justification for undermining people's privacy; a general argument cannot be made that people are physically very safe in exchange for having no privacy.

Secondly, as previously mentioned, the severity of the violation is the degree to which the interest is violated. For example, as previously mentioned privacy can be perceived as consisting of different levels, or even concentric circles around the individual, where the more personal or intimate the information the greater the expectation of privacy and the greater the harm caused when violated (von Hirsch, 2000; Marx, 2004). At the inner most private level is the individual's core, the most personal level concerning their most intimate life, including their own home, private property or clothes, all of which have a long history of being some of the most private spheres as well as being places where an individual is likely to express their most intimate self. A level up, away from the core and becoming less private, is information about the individual and their personal life more generally. For example, addresses, telephone numbers, email addresses, credit card information, health, personal opinions, beliefs, views and interactions with other individuals. At this level Andrew von Hirsch argues that in the social and working world there might be a need for some disclosure, given certain social situations, but individuals are not expected to disclose personal details without a justification (von Hirsch, 2000: 63). Less private again can be the individual's surface information or information they publicly transmit, either willingly or unknowingly, which will often offer little intimate information other than immediate facts, the individual in the street, for example.

For autonomy, while it is arguably never fully realized as people do not have access to perfect information with ultimate reflective capabilities, people can have access to more or less relevant data, be subjected to varying degrees of manipulation or deception, and can possess differing capabilities in different areas of concern. The degree of the violation can therefore depend on the area in the individual's life where the force is applied. For example, a lie which does not directly influence or change the individual's ability to continue with their own set of plans is less harmful than a manipulation or coercion which aims to directly control what decision the individual makes. Or, withholding information on political elites' decisions that shape policies and practices can directly affect an individual's ability to decide how to act as a political agent to a greater extent than information on where politicians spend their leisure time. Equally, people's liberty can vary depending on what constraints are experienced, in what part of their life and for how long. The severity of the violation helps us understand the specific level of harm caused.

In practice this calculation means detailing the level of harm or damage of both the threat and political hack – in terms of its severity, longevity, the number of people it impacts, whether there are secondary or additional side effects or harms caused, if it is systematic or a one off – and the ability of people to consent, waive or forfeit their rights. This should also therefore include other costs such as financial, reputational, damage to systems, information or intimidation. The level of impact of a hack can therefore be examined in terms of the impact of the threat posed, alongside questions on whether a legitimate target is impacted, to determine if the attack is justified or not.

Conclusion

The use of political hacking clearly raises some important ethical questions around who can use political violence and to what ends. For some, hackers act outside the state and so do not have the moral authority to use violence, and that there are no clear and systematic cultural or ethical guidelines for shaping and informing behaviour. However, it has been argued that there are instances where the state has either failed in its role or is a source of a threat in people's lives, and so limiting the right to defend oneself or other is not ethically correct. It has been argued that even states that have extensive established human rights protections in place can fail in specific cases and so justify some form of response from a non-state actor. As such, individuals, groups and collectives can act as ethical agents; they can act to prevent others from violating our core vital interests and that by being outside the state does not automatically discount this. However, hacking is a complicated, multifaceted and fluctuating phenomenon. A variety of agents, acting for a variety of causes with open and fluid opportunities for others to engage makes developing any systematic review incredibly difficult. The Anonymous of today could be different to the Anonymous of tomorrow. However, this ethical framework gives us a place to start: by examining the activities of a hacking agent in relation to a political situation through the distilling of their actions and the mapping of them to our core rights we can start making ethical judgments and statements about their actions as a form of defending people against some of those threats which others have failed to prevent. This can then inform both those on the outside and within on how to react and what the next set of steps should be. This ethical framework is the first step in understanding what an ethical hacker looks like and can form the basis of a new ethical hacker culture.

3

Political Autonomy, the Arab Spring and Anonymous

Introduction

Over their relatively short history, hackers have embarked on a broad range of different political conversations, debates, movements, events and issues, and have used a diverse array of methods ranging from online graffiti, virtual-sit-ins, message dissemination and protest organizing, to distributed-denial of services (DDoS) attacks, secret document leaking, and the launching of viruses, all with the purpose of utilizing their (threat of) coercive power and influence to effect change. Even within a single operation, the tools used and the political agenda sought can flow and change throughout its lifetime, raising a variety of different ethical questions and debates as a result. Given this fluidity it is challenging to create distinct breaks between the chapters focusing only on specific hacking tools. Instead, broad themes based on the general ethos and political objectives sought by the hackers can be established to help categorize and then facilitate the ethical evaluation. This chapter will focus on operations whose purpose is concerned with political autonomy: that is, restoring, protecting or enabling the individual's and social group's ability to act with their autonomy intact and to use that autonomy to act as political beings. This includes operations whose objective is providing for people's rights in expression, association, access to information and political engagement, and, importantly, how cyberspace has come to play a fundamental role in each of their realizations.

Some of the most infamous examples of hacking operations in this area involve those carried out as part of the Arab Spring revolutions between 2010 and 2012, where Anonymous aided the emerging protest movements throughout the region by shutting down government websites through DDoS attacks, and helping dissidents circumvent online censorship by providing 'online care packages' that allowed anonymous online communication and access to information. This included Operation Tunisia, where on 2 January 2010 Anonymous began landing successful DDoS attacks against several Tunisian government websites, including those belonging to the president, prime minister, Ministry of Industry, minister of foreign affairs, stock exchange and the government Internet agency that had been censoring online dissidence. This was followed by Operation Egypt, starting on 26 January 2011, using DDoS attacks on Egyptian cabinet ministers and providing online technologies to aid communications during the protests. And in 2012, Anonymous attacked Syrian government websites to fight government censorship (Greenberg, 2012b). In similar non-Arab Spring examples, Operation Single Gateway involved Anonymous attacking Thai government websites after it was reported that all Internet activity would be routed through a single node that would allow for government monitoring. The attack revealed government officials' personal information and led to the temporary suspension of government websites (Bangkok Post, 2015). In Operation Comelec, Anonymous attacked the Philippine elections commission to promote greater security on its voting machines; and LulzSec released personal voter information to highlight the ease with which the information could be gained (Bueza, 2016; Ong, 2016; Tan, 2016).

As with most political hacks, there is an important 'messaging' element where the hack is designed to draw attention to a particular issue or deliver a message to an audience: political hacking as a form of protest, either directly or to facilitate the ability of others to protest, therefore features strongly throughout all the chapters in this book. However, these cases go beyond civil protest and message awareness. They involve the direct use of political violence as an actual tool to coerce change as a form of direct action. In each of these attacks coercive violence is used to facilitate the realization of online freedoms, to enable protest and as a direct counter to the state's power. For the political hackers, these operations are centred on the argument that such activities are needed to protect or provide for the vital interest people have in their privacy, autonomy and liberty most broadly, and more specifically, how cyberspace has come to represent an essential avenue for enabling political participation, including the ability to express ideas (often of a political nature) or to engage with the polis and its political infrastructure.

However, can such ends justify the damage or harm caused by these hacking operations? Indeed, various arguments can be made regarding the general *prima facie* duty to obey the state and its representatives. The hackers' actions can undermine this general duty by circumventing the protective apparatus of the state while also inflicting damage on state systems and infrastructure. For instance, by providing technology that allows people to operate in cyberspace completely undetected concerns can be raised that they are effectively preventing necessary police, intelligence and national security efforts to locate and stop threats to the political community. Moreover, this technology creates 'warrant proof spaces', where even if there is a justifiable reason to access information on what people are doing online, there is no physical way for state officials to enforce it. Furthermore, the use of DDoS attacks interrupts online systems and prevents people from accessing online information, which runs counter to the general argument, made by hackers themselves, that people have a right to access online information while also disrupting online systems and limiting people's ability to interact with the state. The debate, therefore, is whether, and to what degree, hackers can cause damage to the state when acting to protect people's cyber-information rights. To resolve this, the chapter will start by arguing for the pivotal role cyberspace has come to play in the realization of people's vital interests in autonomy, privacy and liberty, and their ability to engage as political entities. It will then detail the role of hacker collectives such as Anonymous in the Arab Spring revolutions by facilitating the resistance movements' ability to communicate and organize, as well as the hacker's attacks against state infrastructure. It will then argue that it is possible to map these acts of resistance in terms of the political violence spectrum outlined in Chapter 1 in order to understand the impact of these hacks better. This will enable the application of the ethical framework outlined in Chapter 2 so that ultimately the argument can be made that the actions of these hackers were justified; that even given the damage and harm the hacker's operations caused, restoring the widespread and significant loss of online rights can justify their intervention.

(Political) autonomy: freedom of expression, access to information and association

Chapter 2 argued that an individual's vital interests included protecting their autonomy, liberty and privacy. These each represent a fundamental importance in people's lives and need to be maintained at a certain level. In turn, these fundamental interests form the foundation of a bundle of rights that are the means for ensuring one's engagement with other individuals and being able to act as a political agent. Indeed, these various rights are important in both the general sense, in that they have value through all aspects of the individual's life, as well as playing a vital role in enabling the individual's ability to act as a political agent. That is, these subsequent rights create avenues for the individual to act out their political life: to create their own ideas, and share, shape and critically reflect on them with others; to engage with the wider political community and its various structures; and to act as a check on political authority.

Most relevant to cyberspace, this underpins, but is not limited to, the right to free speech and expression, the right to know, to share information and to be informed, the need for oversight and transparency, and the right to associate as people wish (Brison, 1998a: 312). For online activity this places protections around being able to access and share information, to use cyberspace as a place and means for associating with others, and protection against surveillance of online activity. Starting with freedom of expression and access to information, if autonomy is the ability of the individual to conceptualize their own reality with relevant information and pursue it without undue control or interference, then freedom of expression and access to information are vital for both the speaker and the listener. For example, with respect to liberal thought these freedoms have been discussed in terms of their importance in the discovery of truth, with John Stuart Mill arguing that 'if a voice is given to a wide variety of views over the long run, true views are more likely to emerge than if government suppresses what it deems false' (Mill, 1968: 164–5; see also Milton, 1968; Greenwalt, 1989); or in terms of allowing diversity, multiple voices and sources of information protect minorities while allowing for individuals to better reflect on their own understandings (Greenwalt, 1989); or through the argument of distrust, where information and expression prevent any actor from being too dominant (Blasi, 1977; Edstein, 1992); or through the argument for promoting a more tolerant society (Bollinger, 1986; Lewis, 1989); or the pressure release argument which allows people to express themselves and thus promotes a more stable society (Emerson, 1970; Greenwalt, 1989; Strossen, 1990); or a combination of these arguments (Emerson, 1970; Greenwalt, 1989; Cohen, 1993).

Importantly, these various debates point out that while an objective truth might not exist, dialogue and access to information can play critical roles in exploring the variety of truths and encouraging critical reflection through exposure to new information. It empowers the individual's autonomy by allowing access and exposing them to various ideas, truths, details and others' experiences, vital to providing them with the intellectual tools they need to critically reflect on options and make decisions on how they want to live their life. Therefore, an individual with their autonomy intact has information available to them so that they can make informed decisions. Their autonomy becomes hindered if the information is withheld from them, whether it is specific information they require in relation to a specific decision they need to make, or a general access to information to make them overall more informed. It can also play a particular role in enabling the individual to act as a political agent as it highlights the importance of penetrative transparency, active oversight, education, provision of information and the right to know as crucial mechanisms for enabling the individual to be an informed and autonomous political individual (Scanlon, 1972; Baker, 1978; Scanlon, 1979; Dworkin, 1985; Strauss, 1991; Fried, 1992; Post, 1993: 666; Meyers, 1995; Nagel, 1995). As political agents, Habermas argued, it is vital that citizens have access to the public sphere so that they can participate in the creation and shaping of public opinion, and that processes of communicating, sharing and absorbing information are pivotal to this and create subsequent rights to information, expression and association (Habermas, 1996).

Furthermore, there can be additional benefits in increasing social knowledge and the value that freedom of expression has within democracies. Indeed, these information freedoms are vital to preventing the abuse of authority – often in terms of governments, but also for all individuals in positions of authority. That is, 'if those in power are subjected to public exposure for their wrongs in the manner exemplified by journalist accounts … corrective actions can be taken', and 'if public officials know they are subject to such scrutiny, they will be much less likely to yield to the inevitable temptation presented to those with power' (Greenwalt, 1989: 142). Expression and information contribute to the examination of political elites and the sharing of alternative ideas to empower the political process. Freedom of expression and access to information play an essential part in maintaining the wider democratic fabric of society. For example, Cohen argues that freedom of speech is fundamental to the principle of popular and deliberative sovereignty with its demands of 'free and open discussions among citizens' (Cohen, 1993). Restrictions of these rights create 'political inequality between those whose speech is allowed and those who are restricted …. Restricted free speech impedes the free flow of information, perhaps reducing the quality of democratic discussions and decisions' and 'limits the range of ideas and opinions in political discussions' (Fitri, 2011: 4). UNESCO has expressed the importance of these liberties as being actualized through cyberspace, stating that 'free, open and trusted Internet … enables people to not only have the ability to access information resources from around the world, but to also contribute information and knowledge to local and global communities' (UNESCO, 2015: 9).

The right to association is another right based on the more fundamental interest that individuals have in their liberty and autonomy. As a legal concept, it is sometimes considered as a 'shorthand phrase used by courts to protect traditional … rights of speech and petition as exercised by individuals in groups' (Raggi, 1977: 1). Therefore, there are key overlaps between the right to associate and the just discussed right to expression and information, especially when the association is used to convey beliefs and ideas (Raggi, 1977: 3). Again, there is also added value in associating as an important mechanism counterbalancing and limiting the power of authority and the state. However, the right to associate goes beyond the right to expression and by looking at both its autonomy and liberty-based roots this can be seen; as Alexis de Tocqueville stated, 'the right of association therefore appears … almost as inalienable in its nature as the right of personal liberty' (Raggi, 1977: 9).

Possessing the freedom to associate can allow the 'individual to realise his own capacities or to stand up to the institutional forces that surround him' offering the opportunity 'to join with others of like mind in pursuit of common objectives' (Emerson, 1964: 1). Reflecting on the role vital interests play in the individual's life, possessing the liberty to physically associate with those one chooses is essential as a method of making more effective one's needs, aspirations and liberties. Providing people with the necessary information and ability to interact with others plays an essential role in people physically being able to realize their own life goals. While the interest in autonomy recognizes the critical role that association has as a vehicle for discussion, debate and idea-sharing as fundamental to an individual's ability to reflect and explore ideas and information. Being free to associate is therefore an essential manifestation of one's liberty, whereby a person is at liberty to engage in the company of those they choose; while their autonomy is a mechanism for furthering one's understanding and sharing understanding with others; and with the interest in privacy putting restraints on others from unduly impeding on that association and the information it contains within.

Again, association is a specific right for those governed by democratic principles that represent a key mechanism for the individual to become part of the democratic process, though it can also be argued that all citizens have a fundamental right to associate as political beings to practice their political agency as a collective. This is because association allows people to congregate together, both in the real and cyber world, to collectively represent their own interests and create social bonds in light of those interests, or use that congregation to express themselves collectively to others and to the state. In *Sweezy* v *New Hampshire*, Chief Justice Warren explicitly linked political expression and association as fundamental to the control of the government as advocacy, lobbying and joining together behind a particular, common message through the power of an association's collective action can be an important part of countering state power (Raggi, 1977: 8). Similar to free speech, cyberspace has dramatically altered and contributed to the ability of people to associate and has created new, virtual realms and avenues that facilitate this association, which would not be possible otherwise. It cuts across jurisdictions, lowers boundaries, diversifies opportunities, and makes connections that cannot be achieved in any other way.

Cyber-information rights

While the various rights have a long intellectual and political history, cyberspace has come to represent a distinctly new arena for their realization. Indeed, for the debate on political hacking the online space has come to represent one of the most important avenues for people to express themselves, carry out their right to free speech, listen to others and gain access to information. The birth of the modern information nation has dramatically changed how people, organizations and states carry out their everyday lives and activities (Bellaby, 2016). And this dependency is widening as the sheer number of people who have online access is dramatically increasing and reaching across social, economic, geographical and political boundaries. Indeed, the Internet has significantly altered the means and forms of social interaction, creating new ways and methods of communicating and sharing information that would not be possible without cyberspace, and it has become ethically crucial in people's lives. The online space has created a widening of resources for people, making it easier than ever before to share and express oneself to a global audience for an incredibly low cost. It lowers the boundaries for people to access and share information. In an idealized form (as hackers and online activists would argue), cyberspace can offer an unrestrained, unfiltered and fluid system, allowing people the opportunity to share ideas without having to go through existing power brokers. It crosses jurisdictional boundaries in ways and with ease no other form of communication allows. It is increasingly diverse in content, format and author. And it connects people to other people, and people to ideas in ways that would otherwise not be possible (Denning, 1999). Whether it is from the sheer volume of information deposited across websites, through direct online chat functions, or through social media platforms that enable the instantaneous and widespread sharing of all forms of information media, the Internet has become a daily, accessible, easy, widespread and diverse platform of expression, association and information supply in ways that physical media cannot.

As Denning argues, 'the Internet is clearly changing the landscape of political discourse and advocacy. It offers new and inexpensive methods for collecting and publishing information, for connecting, coordinating action on a global scale, and for reaching out to policy makers' and 'supports both open and private communication' (Denning, 1999). For many political hackers, the Internet represents both a means of better securing these rights in the real world, as well as a new space in which these rights can flourish and are in need of protection. As such, cyberspace itself represents a new location that is conceptually open to all, that needs to have its integrity protected from state and corporate unjustified interests. Hacking collectives like Anonymous have thus argued that they are 'against corporations and government interfering on the internet' and that they 'believe it should be open and free for everyone. Governments shouldn't try to censor because they don't agree with it' (Halliday and Arthur, 2010). At the core of much of the rhetoric used by political hackers is the advocacy for 'an overarching belief in freedom of information and in user control of the Internet' (Beyer, 2014: 27). Indeed, Anonymous has come to champion these rights in cyberspace and as such 'attacks on whatever target offended its values, like freedom of speech and anti-corporatism' (Greenberg, 2012b: 183) with a primary focus on free-speech, deregulation and meteoric sentiments (Levy, 1984; Borsook, 2000; Krauth, 2012; Fuchs, 2013; Golumbia, 2013). As Anonymous stated in an early video, 'Hello Internet. I am one Anonymous. Anonymous is a collective of individuals united by an awareness here to promote the truth, promote free speech, stand up against human injustice, we fight corrupt corporations and protest governments who bastardise freedom' (FLSnag, 2011). Such ideals were then further detailed in their 2011 Anonymous manifesto, which argued for the upholding of 'the rights and liberties of its citizens, free from undue influence from those privileged by greater resources, influence and power; to circulate uncensored information in order to guarantee these rights; that citizens should not be the target of any undue surveillance; that privacy is a common interest of humanity; and that it is the responsibility of all citizens to take actions and maintain an open and transparent society' (Anonymous, 2011). Other self-theorizing communicated by the hackers often refers to fighting 'the loss of more liberties such as censorship, phone and Internet surveillance and eminent domain laws' (Kumar, 2011), stopping 'campaigns of misinformation' and the 'suppression of dissent' (Vamosi, 2008).

These cyber-rights can therefore be seen as an important mechanism for signposting the political community, and the state, towards how to provide appropriate space for the individual to flourish online and to protect them from harm through controlling, monitoring and limiting state or corporate cyber-power. It is necessary to hold the state to account in terms of both its own coercive power over the population as well as its obligation to provide the required security in both cyberspace and the real world in terms of information rights (Rawls, 2007: 226). Therefore, rights regarding online activity can have value in protecting the individual from the power of all states generally. That is, while such rights do represent a fundamental attribute of a healthy democracy, these online rights are of fundamental importance for all peoples across all political systems in order for them to properly decide for themselves on how they wish to engage with their polis and prevent undue violations by the state. For political hackers, the debates are therefore centred on using the Internet and cyberspace to express, facilitate and protect these values through file-sharing (including peer-to-peer platforms such as BitTorrent and Pirate Bay); circumventing online restrictions that prevent access to and the dissemination of information across the world wide web; highlighting and gaining momentum behind a particular cause; gaining access to secret information and publicizing it or providing a means for whistleblowers to share their insider knowledge, predominantly national security secrets; or using the Internet and our reliance on cyberspace as a means of carrying out various forms of direct action both in the real world and the cyber world.

Part of the priority for such online freedoms is the protection needed against encompassing data-mining and dataveillance. Data-mining focuses on collecting and collating information across the swathes of digital data stored on different databases about where people live, their phone numbers, physical descriptions, age, medical details, legal transgressions, political party affiliation, place of work, property value, financial documents, and then all this information again on their children and spouses, pooling this information into 'digital dossiers' (Simitis, 1987: 711; Solove, 2004: 1, 4). Dataveillance, meanwhile, involves tracking that information created as a by-product of the individual moving through cyberspace, as almost every online activity creates an electronic footprint or signature that can be found in the ocean of transaction data created in the course of everyday life (Dempsey and Flint, 2004: 1464). For example, websites can track a customer's web-surfing secretly when they access the website, including data about the ISP, computer hardware and software, the website they linked in from and exactly what parts of the website they explored and for how long (Solove, 2004: 23). Both data-mining and dataveillance have therefore gained increased attention from both government intelligence organizations as well as private corporate actors; because of arguments that there are relatively high correlations between personal attributes and behaviour it is a relatively cheap and easy way of understanding and predicting how an individual or a group will act (Hausman and McPhereson, 1996). By collecting information *en masse* the hope is one of 'discovering meaningful patterns in the data' (Gandy, 2003: 28) in order to build profiles of both people and events to create a veritable 'crystal ball' which can be used to understand the individual and predict his intentions (Keefe, 2005: 99). These data-mining and dataveillance efforts by both state and corporate actors can vary in intensity and breadth depending on whom they target and how much information they gather. From precisely targeted searches on specific individuals authorized through a transparent judicial process and limited in scope, to *en masse* drag-net, blanket-type collection where as much data as possible is taken with no oversight or limitations in place. The differences in the type of collection used can then represent different violations of people's online privacy, which can justify different countermeasures as people act to protect themselves.

A spectrum of cyber-interests

What is pivotal, however, is that these rights are not singular or absolute. Across all the rights mentioned there are key debates about what the appropriate limitations should be and what do to when they come into conflict. For example, when free speech becomes hate speech and how to know if and when one limits the other (Greenwalt, 1989; Post, 1991; Schauer, 1993; Brison, 1998b); or when the speech is libellous, fraudulent, defamatory, deceptive, coercive or antagonistic; or when the release of information regarding a political actor's activities is of greater public interest than their right to privacy; or when an association is discriminatory with the aim of causing harm to another. Indeed, hackers from Cult of the Dead Cow noted such limits even in the openness of cyberspace: 'We recognise the right of the government to forbid the publication of properly categorised state secrets, child pornography, and matters related to personal privacy and privilege, among other accepted restrictions' (Ruffin, 2001). Therefore, when two or more vital interests come into conflict, what is needed is an evaluation process to detail the different levels of harm caused by the conflicting interests.

In terms of online rights and interests, this can include detailing the types of information being allowed or restricted: is the information of significant, timely or critical importance, especially in terms of enabling people to act as political agents, so that limiting its access would have a significant impact people's ability to protect or realize a vital part of their life, such as their physical or mental integrity? Or is the information potentially harmful, so that allowing it would cause harm to another? Or does it belong to another, so sharing it would violate their privacy? Or is it biased, propaganda, or intellectually and factually incoherent, and so could violate people's ability to reflect on their decision-making accurately or critically? Equally important is how many people have their access blocked: is it targeted to a select few or *en masse*? Or what level of intimacy does the information gathered represent to an individual? The number of people and the degree to which their online access is controlled, monitored or limited, all needs to be examined as a complex whole, both in terms of the harm caused by the activity of the threatening agent, often the state, and the harm caused by those actions seeking to prevent the threat.

Anonymous and the Arab Spring

One of the most infamous examples of political hacking in this area is the role of hackers like Anonymous and Telecomix in the Arab Spring uprisings. Their first key contribution was playing a part in the early stages of the Tunisian revolution, also known as the Jasmine Revolution, a 28-day campaign of civil unrest and resistance in Tunisia. During this period there were demonstrations against President Ben Ali, who had been in power since 1987, promoted by high unemployment, food inflation, corruption, poor living conditions and the severe lack of political freedoms, notably freedom of expression, which led to his eventual ousting. The protesters themselves had to face the challenge of organizing the protests as well as getting their message out to a broader audience, both within and outside of Tunisia. This was particularly difficult as Tunisia was a heavily censored country, scoring

164 out of 174 in the Reporters Without Borders Press Freedom index (Coleman, 2014: 144). During the revolution the Ben Ali regime used a 'phishing scam, involving malicious script, to plunder the usernames and passwords to the social media accounts of Tunisian activists' in order to track and then shut down their efforts (Coleman, 2014: 166). For Anonymous, it was not until a Tunisian citizen, Shim Amamous, reached out to them hoping 'Anonymous would get involved in publicising the troubles in his country' and 'pitched a proposal' to the collective to 'use Anonymous resources to publicise the plight of the Tunisians revolution' (Coleman, 2014: 174). The result was Operation Tunisia, a series of cyber-attacks and digital resource provisions provided by Anonymous to help facilitate the Tunisian efforts. This included providing software and training Tunisian protestors to evade government censors and coordinate their own movements.

The work of Anonymous also included a successful DDoS attack on 2 January 2011 against several Tunisian government websites, shutting off access to the websites of the president, prime minister, Ministry of Industry, minister of foreign affairs, stock exchange and the government Internet agency that had been censoring online dissidence sites (Hill, 2011a). During this time, Tunisian activists 'flying under the banner of Anonymous organised further protests, and Anonymous in Western countries jumped in to offer technical support', including vital care packages for dissidents that 'provided advice on how to hide their identities on the Internet and developed ... script ... to help evade government phishing campaigns' (Webb, 2021: 177).

Following the success of the social movements in Tunisia, the Egyptian people publicly called for Muhammed Mubarak, who had been the leader from 1981, to step down and organized protests starting on 25 January 2011. When the Egyptians rose up against President Mubarak, Anonymous and Telecomix 'came to their assistance when the government attempted to cut off Internet Access to keep protestors organising and communicating', providing encryption software to evade government censors, launching DDoS attacks on government websites and ensuring that protestor videos were widely disseminated across the Internet (Casserly, 2015). Through Operation Egypt, Anonymous attacked the Egyptian government, starting on 26 January 2011, with DDoS attacks on Egyptian cabinet ministers and again providing online care packages to aid communications during the protests (Greenberg, 2012b). On 28 January the Egyptian government shut the whole Internet off, and 'in order to regain some connectivity Anonymous worked with another hacker crew, Telecomix' to 'figure out how old modems, faxes, and phones could be used to connect circuitously to the Internet' (Coleman, 2014: 192). Telecomix provided Egyptian activists with surveillance evading tools, such as TOR to anonymize digital communications, and built virtual private networks, mirrors and proxies to restore access to blocked content (Owen, 2015: 49). Using a tool called nMap, they 'scanned the entire

Egyptian IP address space to find a few thousand machines that still had access to the Internet and injected human-readable messages into their webserver logs describing how to engage online safely and securely' (Owen, 2015: 48). Telecomix also worked with French Data Network, 'a hacker friendly Internet Service Provider ... to set up hundreds of dial-up modem lines' (Owen, 2015: 49). They also found as many fax lines as they could and 'sent out thousands of leaflets to fax machines of university campuses, cyber cafes and businesses explaining how to get around the blackouts' (Owen, 2015: 52).

Finally, in 2012 Anonymous attacked Syrian government websites to fight government censorship (Greenberg, 2012b). Anonymous carried out 'an exhaustive analysis of the Internet shut-down in Syria and we have concluded that the Syrian regime has physically severed the fibre optics and coaxial cables coming into Syria. Essentially, they have physically "pulled the plug out of the wall"' (Holmes, 2012; see also Musil, 2012). Building on the work done in Tunisia and Egypt, Anonymous had been preparing for this and 'produced and disseminated the Syrian care packages' as well as setting up 'emergency independent media centres ... in every city in Syria' (Lennard, 2012). In the absence of a free press, Anonymous used social media to disseminate information during the uprising to the wider world and to communicate with journalists overseas to ensure there was sufficient media coverage (Holmes, 2012). Telecomix disseminated 'videos and photographs of atrocities committed by Assad's police and military forces. To avoid backlash on those who might be identified as sympathizers if the information was shared through specific social media accounts, Telecomix used a brute force method of sending the information to 'as many Syrian email addresses as they could collect, including addresses of pro-Assad groups and individuals' and sent the following message, 'Dear people of Syria, Fighters for Democracy ... please find attached ...' (Owen, 2015: 51). They also built websites with Internet security guidelines in Arabic and downloadable software containing 'Firefox browser plug-ins, TOR bundle, secure instant messaging software, and a link to the Telecomix IRC' (Owen, 2015: 52). Punkbad discovered logs showing the Internet activity of thousands of Syrians, including 'locations, sites they had visited, and the complete contents of their communications' (Owen, 2015: 52). The logs came from Blue Coat Systems and highlighted the widespread role Western surveillance device manufacturers have in repressive regimes like Syria and Iran. Following their popularized slogan, 'When your government shuts down your Internet, shutdown your government' (Greenberg, 2012b), Anonymous also began a series of attacks on various Syrian government targets hosted outside of the disconnected country, including the embassy websites in China, Australia and Saudi Arabia, and the Baath political party site and Syrian Railway System (Greenberg, 2012b). Most went offline overnight, but were back on by the following day. During this time Anonymous issued several statements expressing its general support for the anti-government protests and emphasizing the importance of online freedoms in all people's lives. Indeed, French Foreign Ministry spokesperson Phillippe Lalliot said that the Syrian communications blackout imposed by officials was of 'extreme concern' as it represented 'another demonstration of what the Damascus regime is doing to hold its people hostage' (Holmes, 2012). Amnesty International said that cutting the Internet could signal that Assad was seeking to hide the truth of harmful activities happening within the country (Holmes, 2012).

Applying the just criteria

These political hacks are focused on protecting people's political autonomy, privacy and liberty by undermining or attacking government institutions and representatives. As discussed, during the Arab Spring, across Operation Tunisia, Operation Egypt and Operation Syria, Anonymous aided the emerging protest movements by shutting down government websites and helping dissidents circumvent online censorship. In Tunisia, 'Ben Ali's government tightly restricted free-expression and political parties' (Anderson, L., 2011: 2), while in Egypt as the protests grew, social media websites were increasingly blocked (Hill 2011b; Woodcock, 2011). These hackers argue for the importance of protecting or providing fundamental online freedoms, such as the right to expression, association and access to information.[1] The arguments made are that given the widespread and significant lack of information rights, the damage caused can be justified.

However, on the other side of the debate is that these hacks caused direct damage to government systems and infrastructure, and DDoS attacks by their very nature limit people's access to information. Indeed, DDoS attacks have received mixed support even within the wider hacker community, given

---

[1] In its very first session in 1946, the UN General Assembly adopted Resolution 59(I), stating, 'Freedom of information is a fundamental human right and … the touchstone of all the freedoms to which the United Nations is consecrated'. In 1995 UN Special Rapporteur on Freedom of Opinion and Expression, Abid Hussain, stated that 'Freedom will be bereft of all effectiveness if the people have no access to information. Access to information is basic to the democratic way of life. The tendency to withhold information from the people at large is therefore to be strongly checked' (UN Doc. E/CN.4/1995/32, para. 35). Moreover, in August 2013 Germany and Brazil led the need for a UN General Assembly resolution based on both the right to privacy online and the right to freedom of expression as outlined in the Universal Declaration and International Covenant on Civil and Political Rights 1966 (ICCPR), arguing that if people are watched online or restricted to what they can access it would significantly violate their vital interest in their own autonomy as they would not be able to express themselves freely (Bauman et al, 2014: 133).

that it goes against the access to information ethos. For instance, Oxblood Ruffin, member of the hacker group Cult of the Dead Cow, argues that DDoS action is 'illegal, unethical and uncivil' censorship, as the goal is to render inaccessible speech on the Internet that has no other outlet (Sauter, 2015: 47), while Gabriella Coleman detailed the internal disagreements within the Anonymous hacker collective over the use of DDoS, both on information principled grounds as well as the negative impact it could have on the overall cause long-term (Coleman, 2014: 91). Moreover, these hacks represent an undermining of the general and automatic obligation to obey the authority of the state and the stability it brings, whether this is based on arguments based on the citizen's role in the social contract; or because of expectations of gratitude or fair play in a system filled with competing personal needs; or because people tacitly or explicitly consent to abide by the same rules; or simply because it is in their own self-interest (Smith, 1973). Indeed, broad arguments can be made that intelligence collection, including online monitoring, does represent a 'significant ethical role ... in the political community' as it is 'needed and depended upon to protect against a range of external and internal threats', and thus places a duty to collect data 'to detect, locate and prevent any threat to the political community' (Bellaby, 2014: 2). When intelligence is used within the appropriate limits and mechanisms to protect society and individuals from harm, there is a general ethical justification that can be made. To resist these efforts is to undermine the authority of the state, the good it represents in people's lives and provides opportunity for other online threats to emerge.

To reconcile this tension, by using the spectrum of political violence outlined in Chapter 1 it is possible to give more detail to the types of resistance these hacks represent and the impact they have. Indeed, 'resistance' as a concept is an umbrella term whose broad definition encompasses a diverse range of activities who at their core refer to the individual or group acting according to their own schema in contradiction to that of some power: to resist is to 'withstand, strive against, or oppose' (Delmas, 2018b: 15); 'acting autonomously in [one's] own interests' (Gregg, 1993: 25); active efforts to oppose, fight and refuse to cooperate with or submit to ... abusive behaviour and control' (Profitt, 1996); 'engaging in behaviours despite opposition' (Carr, 1998: 453); or 'questioning and objecting' (Modighaini and Rachel, 1995: 112). Beyond this core element, however, different acts of resistance can vary greatly. This variation can therefore be matched to the spectrum of political violence outlined in Chapter 1, as different forms of resistance can be spread across it depending on the harm or damaged caused. By looking at resistance across this spectrum one can argue that at the top it can include overt aggressive resistance, with the use of physical and destructive coercion to publicly send a message to those involved, such as armed civil unrest or sabotage. This can then be broken down further depending on the degree of destruction or harm suffered, ranging from inflicting large casualties, to significant destruction of property, to long-term restriction of services, to low-level financial costs, to temporary inconveniences. This leads on to the lower form of overt non-harmful resistance, including activity that is not physically destructive but still actively disseminates an undermining message through a physical act, such as a protest march or occupying some prominent space (McAdam, 1982; Morris, 1984; Robinson, 1995; Dunaway, 1996). In practice this can include public protests such as marches, sit-ins, picket-lines, demonstrations and gatherings whose purpose is to send a message through the public act of speaking out and associating *en masse*, and where causing minor inconvenience acts as a tool to increase the reach and emphasize the political point. Below this are more subtle forms, such as working slow or wearing a badge of support for a particular movement where the damage is low (Scott, 1985; Carr, 1998; Prasdas and Prasad, 1998), or non-destructive covert activity which undermines an authority's general efforts without it ever being aware (Hollander and Einwohner, 2004: 545). For example, failure to perform or the withholding or services or goods to hinder the authority's realization of that task (Razmetaeva, 2014). This conceptualization of resistance as levels can be mapped onto the actions taken by the political hackers to detail their impact so that the ethical principles argued for in Chapter 2 can be applied to determine if these political hacks are justified or not.

The level of political violence: 'online care packages' and DDoS attacks

Hackers, and technologists more broadly, have long worked to develop and share new technologies that circumvent government censorship and online monitoring. These activities all act against the wishes of the state's representative and political elite, often motivated because the government has actively decided to restrict access to cyberspace or because it systematically collects digital data on what people do as part of its general intelligence collection mission.

Such activities can be situated within a wider wave of online resistance and privacy endeavours that have highlighted a split between the desire of the state to monitor and control digital activity, and the rights of individuals to exert their online privacy and autonomy. In China, for example, its 'Golden Shield Project' – also known as the Great Firewall of China – censors online content while also systematically probing for and shutting down any programs that might try to aid access to outside information or the dark web, leading to the development of programs that allow individuals to 'tunnel' through the wall and gain access to outside information (TOR, 2015). Similarly, the development of complex end-to-end encryption in messaging applications such as WhatsApp and Telegram have raised questions in India, where the new 256-bit encryption is far above the officially allowed and much quicker to crack 40-bit encryption, allowing individuals to communicate without others accessing the content (Griffin, 2016). Equally, in the USA in early 2016 this became a very public debate as the FBI and technology company Apple disagreed on the power of the state to force companies to obey their demands in areas of security, as Apple phones' 'auto-delete' function (where if too many incorrect passcodes are entered the data is automatically deleted) prevents brute force cracking by police. Or for online browsing, one of the most renowned tools, TOR, is an easily downloadable program that allows a computer to use the Internet anonymously through onion routing – a form of layered encryption where the traffic is processed through three nodes and encrypted at each stage so that both content and external information about who is the origin or destination of the information is protected.[2] This allows for the anonymous provision and use of various kinds of 'hidden online services' including website hosting denoted by the .onion URL, online messaging, VOIP communications and data sharing.[3] This has resulted in the creation of what is commonly referred to as the 'dark web', the collected sum of these anonymous websites that cannot be found through regular search engines and is only accessible through systems like TOR. On the dark web the IP addresses of the servers and users are hidden, making it very difficult to know who is visiting or behind the sites. The dark web has thus become synonymous with being able to carry out one's activities in cyberspace free from outside monitoring.

The distribution of these online care packages by Anonymous is arguably a form of non-harmful covert resistance that exists at the lower end of the spectrum. Anonymizing software such as TOR and force-attack-proof encrypted hardware are all examples of where the activity itself is limited in terms of direct impact on other people with no intention to directly

---

[2]   The original computer will establish a chain of connections through at least three nodes and will negotiate a different encryption key with each of them to encrypt the electronic message being sent. Once the communication is with a nest of three layers of encryption the message is sent the first node. Each of the nodes will have one of the encryption keys to remove a layer of encryption and will only be aware of who is next in the chain. The message is passed along with another layer being removed and only then discovering who is next in the chain. (Abbott et al, 2007: 2). End-to-end encryption can play an important (though not necessary) part of this communication process as this can add an extra layer of protection by encrypting the information that is being sent to the server at the end of the chain and so can ensure that the message is encrypted to even those at the end node and only accessible to the intended recipient (Reed et al, 1998: 482; Goldschlag et al, 1999; TOR, nd).

[3]   Other tools include Covercast, which is a 'censorship circumvention system that broadcasts the content of popular websites in real time, encrypted videos streams on common live-streaming services such as YouTube' (see McPherson et al, 2016).

undermine the efforts of the intelligence community but rather to secure people's privacy and autonomy. Direct conflict with the authorities is not a necessary or even an essential part. Even if the possession or use of such technology were illegal it is still an act of non-harmful covert resistance – the legality of the act does not change its fundamental nature. Equally, the provision of technology to access the world wide web in and of itself causes no harm or damage to people, infrastructure, services or reputations. It is providing people with access to a source of information that, without further qualification, can be argued to have become an important part of how individuals carry out their digital lives as a means of expressing and maintaining their autonomy and engaging as political beings. The Internet has become a fundamentally important way for people to share ideas, express themselves, gain new information, associate and organize their life, and being able to do these things online has come to play an incredibly important means of carrying out one's political life. Bellaby has argued elsewhere that restrictions to online content can be made in those instances where the website is explicitly and directly facilitating the harming of another, such as 'websites being used to organize, plan or carry out an act of terrorism or to recruit and train potential terrorists' (Bellaby, 2016: 309–10). However, there needs to be the ability to discriminate so that only very harmful sites are blocked. Government censoring seen in these cases are either indiscriminate between the different forms of online content, or blocks content that is politically sensitive, but is not directly harmful. Therefore, the level of harm done directly is arguably very low: no systems are damaged, nothing is taken offline, defaced, altered or removed. No vital interests are harmed, and there are no physical damages to systems, reputations or financial institutions. The negative impact, therefore, is more in terms of the wider activity of resisting the will of the government and its representatives, and given that this government will is an explicit unjustified, *en masse*, indiscriminate and expansive restriction of information freedoms, then the resistance that counters these state efforts are justified.

In terms of justifying the provision of technology which protects people from surveillance, therefore, even given the implication of creating a new 'privacy-plus' space (a warrant proof space where even with legitimate need for intervention the state cannot force itself in) from the point of view of the individual this does not diminish their right to establish privacy protection over their information or to access information as the full-realization of their autonomy. Judith Thomson gives the example whereby if an individual wishes to put something precious to them in a safe to prevent others from looking at it, then it is their right to do so, and indeed represents a clearer demonstration that they wish to stop others from looking at what they own. Breaking into it would be a clear violation of their privacy (Thomson, 1975). Moreover, when individuals lock away their private items it is not done in the knowledge that should the need arise the door can be blown off. It is not the responsibility of the individual – or safe manufacturers – to ensure this option. If we make Thomson's safe crack-proof this does not undermine the individual's right to use it, even to the detriment of possible future intelligence collection. It is the state's duty to demonstrate why such protections for specific individuals should be necessarily pulled down. The individual is assumed innocent until proven guilty and the danger of demanding presumed access to an individual's property flips this; that there is an assumption that they will be guilty of something and so the state will need access; or that using such protections is an inherent indication of future guilt as a form of pre-crime (Solove, 2007a: 748; Zedner, 2007: 265). Any method used by the state that is unable to draw distinctions between who they are harming is unjustified.

The provision of online care packages by Anonymous and Telecomix, therefore, provides individuals and groups the necessary technology to circumvent monitoring of what people do online, important in terms of protecting online privacy as well as autonomy as people are without the panoptic restraint, while also facilitating access to and sharing of information. Therefore, it can be argued that even though anonymizing technology provides a nearly impenetrable barrier, the individual has the right to exert what protections they feel is required to ensure their privacy.

In comparison, there were also actions whose purpose was to directly damage the government's online infrastructure through DDoS attacks, the aim of which was to shut down publicly used websites. In those Arab Spring hacking operations where Anonymous landed successful DDoS attacks, it shut down public government websites and damaged government infrastructure. However, the information was of limited significance to people and the disturbance was temporary. For example, the websites of the president, prime minister, Ministry of Industry, and minister of foreign affairs are predominantly information stores, portals to information about the general function of the various branches of government. The information lost was not of an emergency, time-sensitive or politically vital nature, while loss of functionality for those within the government was also limited. It did not significantly or extensively prevent those branches of government from carrying out either their day-to-day tasks or long-term strategic objectives. The loss of this information did not necessarily threaten people's physical or mental welfare by restricting access to medical information or the location or accessibility of emergency services. It was also not directly relevant or needed for people to act as political agents since, while the websites were politically related, the information was superficial. Up-to-date political information – for example, if people needed to evacuate, or were required to make a political decision or activity – was not relayed on these websites and would more likely be conveyed through other media forms. The 'political voice' of the government is therefore not necessarily hindered. Even the stock exchange websites affected were informative and not part of the actual stock exchange infrastructure. Following from the spectrum of political violence as outlined in Chapter 1, the overall level of political violence therefore could be arguably set as medium-low.

Therefore, while the websites information was temporarily withheld, the damage was still relatively low compared to the larger harm caused by limiting people's freedom of expression. Indeed, looking across these cases there was a widespread, generalized and systematic loss of core civil rights to a very large number of people when they had their access to online information and communications curtailed. The government had significantly prevented people from having access to information, communicating between each other, expressing themselves, or fulfilling both their general and specific political autonomy. Indeed, this desire to protect people's privacy and autonomy was an explicit motivation for the hacker collectives. The language used by Anonymous in its Operation Tunisia reveals and reflects this underlying argument for providing for people's autonomy most broadly, and specifically their political autonomy:

A time for truth has come. A time for people to express themselves freely and to be heard from anywhere in the world. The Tunisian government wants to control the present with falsehoods and misinformation in order to impose the future by keeping the truth hidden from its citizens. We will not remain silent while this happens. Anonymous has heard the claim for freedom of the Tunisian people. Anonymous is willing to help the Tunisian people in this fight against oppression. This is a warning to the Tunisian government: attacks at the freedom of speech and information of its citizens will not be tolerated. (Coleman, 2014: 148)

Anonymous has been watching your treatment of your own people, and we are both greatly saddened and enraged at your behaviour. You have unilaterally declared war on free speech, democracy and even your own people ... we are the angry avatar of free speech. We are the immune system of democracy. (Coleman, 2014: 163–4)

it has come to our attention that the ongoing riots in Tunisia have by and large escaped the notice of reliable western news networks. It is the responsibility of the free and open press to report what the censored press cannot. (Coleman, 2014: 153)

These quotes highlight the core political drive and the underlying vital interests that the hacks were seeking to protect or reinstall, and the methods used are reflective of this intention. The proportional gains of re-establishing these core civil rights significantly outweigh the damage done to the state's authority and the website infrastructure. Furthermore, there was no clear alternative, non-violent avenue available. So while the act of shutting down Internet access in and of itself removed various forms of political engagement, those sites actually targeted by the DDoS attacks were both very much part of the game but were not offering a vital service, for example health care or emergency services. Moreover, as the state is the source of the threat there is no other authority to appeal to or legal route to work through. Therefore, it can be argued that these tools that circumvented government control of cyberspace provided a means to remedy the represented threat. Finally, Anonymous made clear warnings to the governments involved and what the repercussions would be. Therefore, there is a clear justification for action, both at the low level, non-harmful care-package provision level, and the more destructive level of DDoS attacks.

Conclusion

One of the main focuses of political hacking is specifically on cyberspace as a location and vehicle for information rights. Prioritizing freedom of expression and wide access to information has been the core ethos of hackers since the birth of the Internet. For some states, however, this represents a threat to their own stability and across both liberal and non-liberal states there has been an increase in state power and monitoring within cyberspace. This chapter looked at one of the most prominent battlegrounds for this debate, and one of the most extreme examples where states have limited online access and activity. However, it has also shown that the online infosphere does represent a pivotal realm for the realization of people's autonomy, liberty and privacy and so can justify attacks on those states which offer an unjustified set of limits.

4

Leaks: From Whistleblowing to Doxxing

Digital release of privileged information can sit both at the periphery of political hacking as well as being a key part of it, depending on how you see the broader hacking phenomenon and which cases are examined. In terms of whistleblowing and the WikiLeaks and Snowden revelations, for example, they are not inherently cases of political hacking since hacking was not the means of gaining or releasing the information. But there are connected arguments regarding the right to know and the importance of revealing wrongdoing that means they are often discussed in tandem, as well as them spawning specific hacking operations – Operation Payback/Operation Avenge Assange – when governments and corporations moved to restrict the leaked information. In comparison, there are those information leaks that necessarily rely on the political hacker on the outside of an organization gaining access to a network, taking inside privileged information and sharing it more widely. For example, when Anonymous hacked into the private security company Stratfor and copied and placed on a public forum 200 gigabytes worth of data. Part of this involves gaining unauthorized access to a targeted system by 'taking advantage of one of the points of entry into a network', including 'electronic mail, remote logins ... or telnets'. Once inside, the hacker grants themselves privileges that allow them to alter the system's code or steal confidential information (Milone, 2002). These operations represent an updated form of leaking and throw up additional questions about when the hacker can target specific institutions, whether they are justified in breaking into their systems, and then what sort of information releases are allowed. Finally, there are also information releases that concern private individuals, whereby a person's personal information is collected and shared publicly.

To evaluate these different types of information releases, this chapter will detail the underlying ethical arguments for leaks most broadly, as this, in turn, shapes how both the retaliation hacks as well as penetrative information gathering hacks are to be judged. To help classify the discussion, those information leaks involving insiders using their privileged position to collect and then distribute information will be referred to as whistleblowing.[1] In comparison, those instances where an outsider gains access to internal information and shares it widely will be referred to as 'doxxing' (a neologism originating from a spelling alteration of the abbreviation 'docs', a shorter version of 'documents'). This will include 'institutional doxxing' when referring to organizations or corporations having their internal documentation shared, and 'individual doxxing' when referring to a person's personal information being shared. This chapter will set out the relevant ethical issues in order to then evaluate the most prominent case examples. It will argue that when a leak reveals sufficient wrongdoing or pertains to information where there is a right to know, often involving information of a political nature, and that the act of leaking does not cause direct harm to another, there are instances where both whistleblowing and doxxing can be justified.

Blowing the whistle on wrongdoing

As a practice, whistleblowing relies on those who work on the inside of an organization who witness some form of wrongdoing and deliberately disclose that information with the view of receiving some form of response, with traditional arguments supporting it often pointing to the value of sharing information on wrongdoing with the public in order to prevent, stop or punish the harm or damage being caused (DeGeorge, 1981; Bowie, 1982; Jensen, 1987; Near and Miceli, 1995; Davis, 1996; Hersh, 2002). Indeed, whistleblowing has been used to expose financial scandals,[2] poverty creating corruption (Carr and Lewis, 2010), and to ensure correct professional practice for medical personnel (Hunt, 1995; Wilmot, 2000; Bolsin et al, 2011), engineers (Fleddermann, 1999; Lynch and Kline, 2000; Harris et al, 2005; Bouville, 2008), and lawyers (Dunfee and Maurer, 1992; Breslin and Dooley, 2002; Mahat, 2008). Transferring this framework across onto national security practice, however, has proven problematic. Indeed, national security whistleblowing is often discussed in terms of betrayal against

---

[1] Terminology on 'leaks' as compared to 'whistleblowing' can vary across the literature. Here leaks are the broad umbrella categorisation for all information released including accidental and purposeful. Whistleblowing is intentional by someone on the inside who uses their position to share information. Neither is intended to give any ethical assumptions about the character of the information release (Johnson, 2003: 3–4; Zelizer and Allan, 2010: 68).

[2] For example, the Bank of Credit and Commerce International (BCCI); Enron, see Sterling, 2002; Jeter, 2003).

both one's institution as well as the nation as a whole, and is criticized for significantly undermining the entire security apparatus (Hoffman, 1984; Bok, 1985; Brenkert, 2010). Within the field of national security and intelligence any whistleblowing culture has been strongly discouraged by fostering a highly closeted nature and a mentality of the privileged position of national security. This has meant that any information leaked has been framed in terms of treason or espionage, limiting debate and preventing any room for whistleblowing as a viable means of oversight. Indeed, existing whistleblowing laws explicitly exclude national security and limit those on the inside to restrictive, and often politicized, mechanisms for highlighting wrongdoing.

Despite this, it will be argued that rather than being excluded from whistleblowing, national security has a heightened need that includes an obligation on behalf of those on the inside to release information when they are aware of wrongdoing. The core of this obligation is drawn from the broad argument that individuals have a duty to prevent harm from being caused to others. This is often framed in terms of the 'Good Samaritan' argument, whereby 'one ought to help, or at least offer to help, those whose welfare is endangered' if there is a minimal cost to oneself (Kleinig, 1976: 385). Indeed, we normally assume that if we can save a human life at minor cost we are obligated to do so. Though Richard DeGeorge goes further in this argument, stating that 'It is not implausible to claim both that we are morally obliged to prevent harm to others at little expense to ourselves, and that we are morally obliged to prevent great harm to a great many others, even at considerable expense to ourselves' (DeGeorge, 1990: 214). Indeed, John Rawls' 'original position', the classical utilitarian's 'sympathetic spectator', or the Golden Rule, each outline how, after we put ourselves in the shoes of those in trouble, we would want the help and creates an obligation to act (Mack, 1980: 235; Rawls, 1977: 111, 152; Smith, 1976: 9);[3] or that the need to stop harm being done is seen as being no different to acting to cause others harm (Feinberg, 1984: 166). Candice Delmas also extensively examines such obligations in terms of (un)civil disobedience, arguing that 'Resistance to injustice is, I will argue, our political obligation' based on

---

[3] There is an extensive literature regarding the expectations of the good or minimal Samaritan (Singer, 1972; Gewirth, 1978; Smith, 1990; Copp, 1991; Whelan, 1991). While in the Anglo-American legal systems there is no general duty to come to the rescue of another (see Rosenbaum, 2004). This usually refers to situations where there is not prior relationship – either from role obligations or causal link – which is not which is being discussed here. Moreover, in Continental European courts anyone who fails to come to the assistant in danger can still be found as both civil and criminal liability. For example, failure to provide assistance is an offence in France according to Article 223–6 of the Criminal Code and in Germany according to section 323c of the Strafgesetzbuch.

principles of justice, fairness, a Samaritan duty, and the duty one owes one's wider political association (Delmas, 2018b: 5).

Indeed, at the most general level all individuals have a duty not to cause others harm through their (in)actions, where all must take reasonable care in their acts or omissions so as not to cause harm to others proximate to them (Atkin, 1932). Further to this, certain relationships (created and defined by our roles, ranks or professions) hold those involved to additional standards of care and duty to act (Horsey, 1994: 974, quoting *Hun v Cary*, 82 N.Y. 65, 71 (1880)). These include specific 'professional negligence' obligations determined by one's profession and caregiving roles, which establish ethical duties and whose members are expected to have higher than average abilities, knowledge or training.[4] And there is also a particular duty to aid those harmed when the actor has himself created a hazardous condition or action that can or does harm others.[5] Indeed, if one's (in)actions negatively impact another then this creates a bond between those actors that places a burden on them to act.

Moreover, for officials within state organizations – and especially national security actors such as intelligence agencies – there is more than a general obligation to act, and a very specific one. The ethical end of the state is to protect and provide for the political community. When looking at the ethical justification of intelligence, for example, it draws its value (even when it causes harm) from its overall role of protecting the political community from threats. That is, given that the ethical justification for the use of intelligence is the protection of the political community, when they not only fail to meet this standard but directly cause the undermining of this, then they fail the very reason for their existence and lose the normal justifications and protections around their secrecy and activity. Depending on the nature of the wrongdoing, therefore, there can be an obligation for the information to be revealed. This normative value can then be extended to those who facilitate the reveal, including acting in defence of those blowing the whistle and releasing this information.

---

[4] Indeed, in legal terms the Bolam Test, established in *Bolam v Friern Hospital*, sets down how those acting as professionals providing services – from surveyors and estate agents to doctors, solicitors, accountants, financial services providers, information technology professionals, patent agents – are to be judged by the standards of their profession as a whole and the duties of care they have towards particular individuals. *Bolam v Friern Hospital* (1957) 1 WLR 583. The duty of care also includes the more specific duties of professional rescuers – such as in doctors or lifeguards – to aid those in harm's way or have been harmed. *Lowns v Woods* (1996) Aust Torts Reports 81–376 (NSW Court of Appeal); *Horsley v Maclaren (The Ogopogo)* (1971) 22 DLR (3d) 545 (SCC).

[5] *Sutherland Shire Council v Heyman*, 1985; *Ticehurst v Skeen*, 1986; The Occupiers Liability Act 1984 introduced a duty of care to non-invited visitors.

However, this obligation can vary depending on the circumstances. For example, there might be a general obligation for those on the 'inside' of the organization witnessing and possibly even partaking in the wrongdoing to act, but if they are to face significant harm personally as a result then this obligation can be mediated. Equally, outsiders do not have an obligation to penetrate an organization and release information. Nor do they have an obligation to facilitate the leak. But there could be a right. Therefore, this obligation should be examined in terms of the potential backlash any whistleblower might face. Indeed, whistleblowing has historically been shown to carry a significant degree of harm for the whistleblower themselves. Retaliation against whistleblowers has been reported in the literature across a range of instances and societies. Philip Jos, Mark Tomkinson and Steven Hays reported that 60 per cent of the whistleblowers they surveyed answered that they were fired or forced to retire (Jos et al, 1989); while Joyce Rothschild and Terance Miethe reported that this was the case for 69 per cent of their survey, with 84 per cent of participants reporting suffering from anxiety or depression as a result (Rothschild and Miethe, 1999); and Joseph McGlynn and Brian Richardson detail how the possibility of slander, physical intimidation and death threats is very real for those who blow the whistle (McGlynn III and Richardson, 2014). In terms of blowing the whistle this means that if there are going to be clear repercussions for the whistleblower then this can act as an intervention on the individual's obligation to reveal. If the impact on the whistleblower is too great then the demand that the individual acts is mediated and there is only a right to blow the whistle rather than an obligation. If, however, the harm being caused is extreme, then it can be argued that the backlash facing the whistleblower can be outweighed, and the obligation resumes. This means that if the blowback is high and the individual's responsibility is low then it can be argued that their obligation to act is mediated – though they still have the right to act if they so wish. If, however, the level of harm being caused by the national security actor were high then the blowback would have to be significant (truly life-threatening for example) to mediate the obligation. The higher the harm and the higher one's responsibility the greater the obligation to act would be.

The value of being informed

A second justification for releasing information rests on the argument that at the general level there is a right to be informed when the information is pertinent to an individual's ability to act autonomously and to act as a full political agent. As previously discussed, for an individual to be able to carry out their autonomous life they must be able to make decisions based on their own designs, with the relevant information and free from undue influence. This means not only should an individual, *all other things being equal*, not be lied to as their decisions are forced to be based on the reality the lie creates, they also need access to the relevant information for their decision-making so that they can critically reflect on their options. Therefore, withholding information means people are unable to make a fully informed rational decision, and are forced to act based on the will of those withholding. Secret-keeping can violate an individual's autonomy as they are unable to decide how to make decisions regarding the world around them and those they interact with and are unable to decide how they should react.

This becomes a strong need to be informed when dealing with one's interaction with one's polis and acting as a political agent. Such a position argues that 'The public, as sovereign, must have all information available in order to instruct its servants, the government ... otherwise ultimate decision making by the people, to whom that function is committed, becomes impossible' (Emerson, 1976: 14). While this argument is often reserved specifically for democracies and the value they place on political engagement, the underlying argument can be made for all political systems whereby all individuals have a right to have the option to be suitably informed in regards to their political community and political authority so they can determine their own political actions. Secrecy limits access to information and in doing so undermines people's role in relation to their political community. This means that distinctions can be made between information on other people generally and information relating to one's political environment. With the former, while it might be interesting to know or might improve one's calculations slightly to know what one's neighbours are doing, on balance the extra information is not going to make a significant improvement in a vital area of one's life (especially when positioned in relation to their neighbour's interest in privacy). The latter, however, refers to information about one's political representatives, institutions or practices that could have a profound impact on one's ability to make a decision or is in a more pivotal area of their autonomous life because it pertains to them acting out their political agency.

There is also a recognition that government decision-makers, like all humans, are fallible. For this reason, public scrutiny is the most effective check on individual shortcomings, a point made by John Stuart Mill: 'The only stimulus which can keep the ability of the body itself up to a high standard is liability to the watchful criticism of equal ability outside the body' (Mill, 2005: 138). Again, this places a particular emphasis on democracies, though similar arguments can also be made for individuals in non-democracies, in that withholding pertinent information is a natural ill as it allows for abuse of power, corruption, incompetence, personal bias, negligence and incumbency to pervert the political process (Stiglitz, 1999: 125; Thompson 1999; Shapiro, 2003; Chambers, 2004; Kono, 2006).

This is particularly important in systems or organizations that emphasize a high degree of secrecy, most notably the intelligence community and other national security actors, as this secrecy creates an internal culture that separates those on the inside from the rest of the political sphere and allows them to feed on this desire for secrecy to create a need for hyper-secrecy. On the one hand, some degree of secrecy around critical areas such as intelligence practice and undercover work is ethically justified when it is done to protect the political community. This is not a call for complete transparency. Secrecy does play an essential role in facilitating the intelligence community's ability to protect both the individual and the political community, for example. However, it also needs recognizing that overly secretive environments or cultures that are placed above or outside the normal political sphere isolate their members and their structures, separating them from those on the outside who are unaware and unable to engage, and so not able to act as a counter and reference point to the internal cultures, and promotes an escalation in the severity of policy and practices. Those on the inside are subjected to a process of in-group/out-group differentiation that dehumanizes 'others', and when coupled with a lack of outside input there is no means of measuring one's moral compass (Bandura, 1999: 194). As a result, officers learn to exclude those considered as outsiders from their universe of obligation (Fein, 2007: 11). Cognitive restructuring means violence or harm is redefined as honourable, for a greater abstract good, and becomes increasingly socially and morally acceptable to those inside (Bandura, 1986: 376). Secretive environments normalize this process, feeding upon itself to reinforce both the need for greater secrecy and a lack of regard for the negative consequences for those on the outside. In such an environment internal criticism is limited as it is seen as a betrayal to the group and so restricts alternative analysis as group mentality smothers dissenting points of view (US Senate Select Committee, 2014: 2). The insular atmosphere skews one's ability to evaluate one's activity. Indeed, Hannah Arendt highlighted how the mandate to try and protect the political community from threats actually encourages them to move further from that ethical end (Arendt, 1979: 423). It is not that those within the intelligence community and their authorizing political actors are necessarily acting according to some private or nefarious agenda, but rather that the prioritizing of a narrow conceptualization of security coupled with a secretive and isolated culture can result in activities being disconnected from the actual interests or needs of those it seeks to protect. This can distort policy application, promoting distrust not only between individuals and the state but also between different social groups, having real repercussions for individuals in terms of social mobility and treatment (Merton, 1968: 477; Simitis, 1987: 719; Kennedy, 1997; Harris, 1999; Robinson, 2000; Harris, 2002; Lever, 2005). This, therefore, underpins not only the argument that wrongdoing in this environment removes the ethical justification for the secrecy as national security agents become the source of the threat rather than protecting people from threats, but also the value of external agents being informed to act as a mechanism for ensuring efficient and suitable behaviour.

The calculation therefore is a combination of how relevant the information is to the decision-making an individual is or should be making, and the area in their life in which the decision is being made. That is, how much more capable will the individual be with the additional information, and is it in an area which is likely to have deeper or wider implications on them pursuing their needs or suffering future harm.

Who to infiltrate

One key update to the classic whistleblowing leaker is understanding if and when those on the outside should penetrate an organization to gain access to the information and then release it to the wider public. Coleman refers to such actions as 'public interest hacks' whereby a computer network is 'infiltrated for the purpose of leaking documents that will have political consequence' (Coleman, 2022). The underlying logic of releasing information still stands, where the justification of the action is judged on the wrongdoing it seeks to alleviate through public exposure, or the degree to which the information is necessary for the individual's important decision-making. However, such actions raise additional concerns, as those on the outside do not inherently have the same awareness of what is going on inside an organization and therefore do not have the same awareness to act as evidence in the justification for their subsequent penetrative actions. The question, therefore, is whether they have the right to break into a system and take the information that is not theirs and then distribute it widely.

In answering this question it is important to distinguish between legitimate and illegitimate targets by building a case based on what information they do have access to, which can then justify the initial penetration. Traditionally, the distinction is between illegitimate targets who themselves are harmless or non-threatening – those who have done nothing to warrant being targeted – and legitimate targets who have acted in some way to represent a threat or to waive their normal protective rights so that they have 'something about them' to justify them being targeted.[6] That is, certain institutions or individuals make themselves legitimate targets when they act in such a way as to waive or temporarily suspend their normal protective rights or when they act in a threatening way (Walzer, 2000: 145). Acting in a threatening manner is relatively straightforward as it builds on the argument made in Chapter 2, that people have the right to act in self-defence and that one

---

[6] Nagel argued the idea that it is not fair to target just anyone in war, there must be 'something about them' in order to justify it (Nagel, 1986: 162).

can attack those who represent a threat pre-emptively to prevent the danger to their wellbeing from being realized. In addition to this, actors can waive their usual protections by 'joining the game', and in doing so knowingly take on a specific role that marks them as a legitimate target (Pfaff and Tiel, 2004: 7). These actors demarcate themselves as separate from the ordinary and sacrifice some of their rights in the process (McMahan, 2006: 381). This can include joining the national security infrastructures given its coercive power over individuals and the knowing choice to be in an industry which involves such risks to themselves. In a system where information is king, politicians can also represent a legitimate target by presenting themselves as subject to scrutiny in terms of the need of the public to fulfil their political autonomy. Beyond this core of the national security and political infrastructures, the current privatization and industrialization of security means that threats have come to include private actors involved in security-related activity – such as surveillance – or directly engage and support critical infrastructure. In this instance, those companies that specialize, work or support security endeavours can be legitimate targets. They might not be 'armed' and possess the coercive and explicit violent power of the state, but they are to some extent engaged in activities that can be 'threatening and harmful' (Walzer 2000: 146; see also Coates, 1997: 236; Slim, 2002: 188).

For those on the outside, it is hard to know the type of legitimate target a target represents until they have been investigated, by which point the hack has already harmed them. This, therefore, presents a particular challenge, especially as self-defence arguments are often presented as imminent and severe, such as Judith Thomson's innocent who is about to be run down by a truck, with the threat very nearly upon them, so that the probability of the threat materializing is high and there are no opportunities for less harmful counterattacks (Thomson, 1991: 283). However, imminent death is not always helpful when looking at secretive threats that are widely, slowly or incrementally but still significantly violating people's vital interests. As a result, the self-defence literature distinguishes between 'self-defence against present definite threats ... definite future threats ... as well as indefinite potential threats' (Lee, 2018: 346; Walzer, 2000). And as argued in Chapter 2, even low-level threats can justify a suitably level of response. Therefore, it is possible to think of the hack as a form of proportional pre-emptive or preventive self-defence, and as such there are varying degrees, times and circumstances which exist and alter depending on whether an institution, corporation or individual can be targeted or not. This means there can be a spectrum or graduation in terms of whether someone is a legitimate target for an appropriately related form of hack. That is, depending on the level of evidence available, the level of threat or degree to which they have waived their protective rights, the level of harm allowable in the political hack changes. The line that distinguishes between legitimate and illegitimate targets is dependent on the extent the actor represents a threat or the extent he has acted to waive his normal protective rights. This requires some evidence to support the idea that they are in fact representing a threat, but for low-level hacks this can include examining their history, actions, rhetoric and relationships. The more known about the target, the more concrete evidence there is, the greater the justification there is for a more impactful form of political hacking. This type of distinction is important because infiltration hacking does not exist in the same temporal immediacy as defending oneself against an imminent blow. But this proportional approach includes using what is knowable through non-harmful means to detail the level of threat and the degree to which it is reasonable to assume the threat is real.

These political hackers must therefore possess some initial information to act as evidence to justify their further hacks to collect more justifying evidence. For example, open-source collection needs no justification but can form the basis of determining the threat represented by an actor. This can provide the evidence needed to act as a justification. This notion of levels of evidence is itself nothing new. Various legal systems mark out levels of evidence, or 'burdens of proof', which are required when assessing whether certain actions are permissible or not. Legal canons draw a distinction between a *reasonable suspicion,* a *probable cause,* a *balance of probabilities, clear evidence,* and *beyond any reasonable doubt,* whereby depending on the circumstances the level of proof required changes. These different levels of probability provide, what Polyvious Polyviou calls, the 'best compromise' between two often opposing interests, 'the intrusions upon the individual and the security of the state' (Polyviou, 1982: 97). Often the political hacker must engage with the evidence available and determine what action is best, given the range of possibilities. Therefore, actions that cause a low level of harm can be used to collect information with only a 'reasonable suspicion' that the threat exists. If the information collected proves fruitful it can be used as further evidence for the justification of those activities which cause a greater level of harm.

This also means that the information, once accessed, needs to be assessed and should not be revealed if the suspicion turns out false. The investigation becomes unjustified once the box is opened and it turns out there is no threat present. In such a case this also means that efforts should be made to rectify the intrusion: accounts made secure, information returned and copies taken destroyed, for example. If, however, there is wrongdoing discovered it can justify a wider reveal.

Knowing what and when to leak

Making the calculation of what and when to leak information means accounting for the overall costs and benefits involved, including the benefit brought about by the revealing of the information (and hopefully remedying the wrongdoing or aiding in people's political autonomy), which can be put in contrast to the potential backlash to the leaker, the and harms/damages done to the target by violating their privacy, and any subsequent harms that revealing the information can then cause.

For instance, those benefits that support the leak will mainly come from preventing the harm done by the activity, policy or practice. This could include, for example, the number of specific harms caused by the activity in question that is violating an individual's or people's privacy, autonomy, mental and physical integrity, or liberty; or broader harms to society such as the degradation of social cohesion if the practice involves the segregation or marginalization of specific sectors of society; and whether the individual will be able to make a more informed decision in a vital area of their life, especially if the information is likely to change their behaviour or how they make decisions in relation to their political authority.

The costs, on the other hand, could include those associated with undermining the ability of the target to successfully continue with their objectives and maintain their expectation of privacy. In terms of national security this can range, for example, from very specific and severe harms such as revealing the identity of an operative who is trying to infiltrate a violent organization and putting them and their family in immediate danger while losing the future intelligence assets that he had been cultivating, to revealing a set of practices that means opponents can create countermeasures that broadly undermines the national security activity. In private organizations the negatives could include disclosing intellectual property to a competitor or promoting a backlash against their employees.

WikiLeaks as ethical whistleblowing, a prelude to a retaliatory hack

In terms of a hacker's role in whistleblowing, as already noted, leaking internal and privileged information is not necessarily new, nor does it inherently rely on hackers. Revelations on the scope of US political and military involvement in Vietnam was publicly exposed in the Pentagon Papers thanks to Daniel Ellsberg, and the Watergate scandal that toppled the presidency of Richard Nixon was helped into the light by the secret FBI informant Mark Felt, known as Deep Throat, who aided *Washington Post* reporters Bob Woodward and Carl Bernstein. These pivotal exposures were achieved well before the rise of the political hacker. However, what political hackers and cyberspace has significantly changed is that state and corporate secrets can be now accessed, smuggled out and eventually leaked with ever greater ease and wider distribution. Large amounts of data can be stored on very small devices, and then the Internet allows for these large swathes of official documents to be shared across the globe at a much lower cost, and once put out into the world it becomes an impossible genie to put back.

Moreover, while neither WikiLeaks nor Snowden's releases required hacking tools to gather and share the information, following the release, political hackers such as Anonymous did act when the US government and corporations moved to limit the ability of WikiLeaks to act as a secure place to deposit and share national security secrets by restricting their funding. Arguments made by the US establishment were based on the premise that the leak itself was unjustified. Therefore, the ethical quality of those hacking operations which sought to restore the ability of WikiLeaks are also directly linked to the ethical justification to release that information. The questions, therefore, are what right WikiLeaks had to reveal national security secrets, whether the state was subsequently justified in putting pressure on private companies to restrict funding and then whether those companies were right to comply, and whether the hackers' response was therefore justified or not.

WikiLeaks itself was set up as an electronic drop-box with 'military grade encryption protection' that would allow potential whistleblowers a place to deposit information, keep their identity secret, even from WikiLeaks, and offer an 'censorable' tool to allow the ethical release of documents (Thorsen et al, 2013). Chelsea Manning (then known as Private Bradley Manning) was a United States army officer stationed in Iraq with privileged access to confidential government information who amassed some 750,000 documents and cables and leaked them to WikiLeaks (Elliott, 2013: 78). Unsurprisingly, the US response to the leak was severe and widespread. Senator Joe Liberman declared it 'an outrageous, reckless and despicable action that will undermine the ability of our government and our partners to keep our people safe' (Lopez, 2010). Lieberman 'reached out to Amazon … and asked it to ban WikiLeaks from its servers' and 'It acquiesced' (Coleman, 2014: 120). Financial firms would follow suit shortly after. In December 2010, WikiLeaks came under intense pressure to stop publishing secret US diplomatic cables, and corporations such as Amazon, PayPal, BankAmerica, Swiss bank PostFinance, MasterCard and Visa froze their customers' donations to WikiLeaks due to political pressures. Manning was sentenced to 35 years in US military imprisonment.

Equally unsurprising, Anonymous was 'outraged', and 'two weeks later, AnonOps became ground zero for the single largest digital direct action campaign the Internet … had ever witnessed' (Coleman, 2014: 120). As part of the wider Operation Payback, Anonymous launched a significant distributed-denial of services (DDoS) attack, organized against PayPal, MasterCard and Visa in 2010 'in response to their decisions to suspend all donations to the online media outlet WikiLeaks due to its unauthorised bulk publication of classified US government documents it received from Bradley Manning' (Adams, 2013). The impact included PayPal being out of services for four days. PayPal ultimately released the pending donations to WikiLeaks, but suspended their account and refused to process new donations (Adams, 2013). Anonymous then issued Operation Avenge Assange (as an expansion of Operation Payback), where hacks were directed against these corporations in response to their limiting access to information.

On the one hand, it can be argued that protecting national security information is both necessary and justified. In many instances, the job of national security actors, whether they be military, diplomatic or intelligence, is about working against the efforts of other states to prevent harm to the political community. These efforts can – and in terms of military action and intelligence activity necessarily do – cause harm to others in pursuing these ends, but this is justified harm in terms of protecting individuals and the political community. Many of these activities are also inherently secretive, and whose secretiveness is ethically valuable as using secretive methods is vital to detect, locate and prevent threats from becoming a reality. Such allowances are ethically justified when done to protect the political community from harm, with appropriate limits in place. On the other hand, however, reports of abuse at detention centres such as Guantanamo Bay and Abu Ghraib, the pervasive growth and unjustified use of technological surveillance, and the increased attention on the use of torture for intelligence collection have all highlighted not only the power of the intelligence community, but also the likelihood of that power being abused. Information about these events was not revealed by intelligence organizations themselves (Finn, 2009; Baldino, 2010; Mazzetti, 2015).

The WikiLeaks releases reported significant abusive behaviour and cover-ups by both military and political actors, as well as highlighting that the legality of some operations was thinner than initially reported (Wells, 2004: 1195; Elliott, 2013: 78; Thorsen et al, 2013: 105). The Afghan War Logs, for example, revealed military accounts of civilian killings that contradicted official public reports given at the time. Indeed, on 17 June 2007 five rockets were fired by a new US weapon on a religious school that failed to kill the target, a senior al-Qaida fighter, and resulted in the deaths of seven children. This tragedy became a scandal, and the Special Operations Command News Service reported at the time that the operation had been carried out by 'Afghan and Coalition forces' after confirming 'nefarious activity' at the site. However, the War Logs revealed this testimony to be misleading. The logs stated that the operation was in fact carried out by a covert troop of US soldiers known as Task Force (TF) 373, whose activity was largely unknown, and the rocket attack had been carried out in the hope that the top-listed target was on the premises. The War Logs revealed this activity for the first time, allowing greater judicial and political investigations into TF 373, and many other instances of civilian deaths (Leigh and Harding, 2011: 117). The Iraq War Logs also revealed extensive secrecy by the UK and US governments regarding statistics on the number of civilians that died in relation to the war. Both governments had previously refused to admit how many ordinary Iraqis had been killed in the conflict, claiming that no official casualty statistics existed except for US and allied soldiers. The leaked War Logs revealed that statistics did indeed exist, and that 66,081 Iraqi civilians had been killed since the records belatedly started in 2004 (Leigh and Harding, 2011: 129). After being analysed alongside other databases, the documents were able to reveal 15,000 civilian deaths beyond the previously known death toll. The two governments had denied the existence of these statistics.

There were also examples of the United States government being engaged in unlawful or undiplomatic activity, undermining both domestic and international codes of conduct central to international politics. Cable 219058, spotted by Germany's *Der Spiegel*, revealed that the United States state department (on behalf of the CIA) had ordered its diplomats to spy on senior UN officials and collect their 'detailed biometric information'. They were also told to go after 'credit card account numbers, frequent flyer account numbers; work schedules and other relevant biographical information' (Leigh and Harding, 2011: 178). The cable had been signed off 'CLINTON', and essentially revealed the United States to be spying on the UN and its secretary-general, Ban Ki-moon. While this type of activity could be expected against terrorists or rogue states, it is not expected against the UN as the forum for international cooperation and exchange, and constitutes a significant breach of three of the founding treaties of the UN.[7] Such activities represent a threat to the security of the state as it both undermines the position of the state in international affairs while also threatening the institution of diplomacy itself as states are less likely to trust, cooperate, communicate and act honestly if they feel their actions are being monitored by one power. This undermines the role diplomacy has in ensuring national security for the state.

The benefits of releasing the information, therefore, includes the ability of the political community to make informed decisions about the foreign policy decisions of their political and military elite as well as bringing to light some significant wrongdoing. For example, the diplomatic cables on the Russian Federation 'painted a bleak and despairing picture of a kleptocracy centred on Putin's leadership, in which officials, oligarchs and organised crime are bound together in a "virtual mafia state"', which when read together 'offered a rare moment of truth-telling about a regime normally accorded international respectability' (Leigh and Harding, 2011: 216). The *New York Times* defended its decision to publish the details by arguing that 'The cables

---

[7]   The UN has asserted that bugging the secretary-general is illegal, citing *The 1946 Convention on Privileges and Immunities of the United Nations* Section 3, Section 30, *The 1961 Vienna Convention on Diplomatic Relations Article* 22.2; Article 27.2; Article 29; Article 30.2.

tell the unvarnished story of how the government makes its biggest decisions, the decisions that cost country most heavily in lives and money … it would be presumptuous to conclude that Americans have no right to know what is being done in their name' (*The New York Times*, 2010). Moreover, while there were criticisms that such revelations were an embarrassment to the US government (Rangarajan, 1998, 18–24; *The Economist*, 2011), in January 2011 Reuters reported that top US diplomats had admitted that the fall-out of the diplomatic cables 'had not been especially bad' (Leigh and Harding, 2011). Even by 2013, there was still no evidence that any individual had been killed as a result of the publication of the files (Elliott, 2013: 82).

Following this, the underlying justification for the WikiLeaks releases is that there was significant degree of wrongdoing, and the information was of key public interest and did not reveal any specific information that put an individual operative's life in danger. The value of the leak is such that when government representatives moved to punish WikiLeaks, without any wider social mandate to do so and given the wrongdoing it was highlighting, then moves to counter these actions of the state can be justified. That is, there is no compelling reason to reissue the secrecy of the information, while there is value in its release. The underlying arguments against revealing the information was that it would threaten the security of agents and missions, yet no sensitive operational material was shared. Indeed, as former Solicitor-General Erwin Griswold notes, 'to any person who has considerable experience with classified material that there is massive over-classification and that the principal concern of the classifiers is not with national security, but rather with governmental embarrassment of one sort or another' (Ambinder and Grady, 2013: 6; see also Griswold, 1989; Wells, 2004: 1203). Government embarrassment, however, is not a justification for keeping something secret when it is their wrongdoing being revealed.

Institutional doxxing: public interest hacks

Institutional doxxing refers to the political hacker breaking into an organization's network, collecting and then distributing their internal data publicly. Recent examples include, 'hacks against security or intelligence firms like HBGary, Stratfor, Hacking Team and FlexiSpy' that were 'orchestrated by hacktivists who explicitly sought to expose wrongdoing' (Coleman, 2022). But other examples also include accessing the email accounts of politicians, such as the case of Sarah Palin, or government institutions, such as accessing and releasing internal police documents.[8] The

---

[8]   In this instance Sarah Palin is seen as an institution rather than an individual, given her political role.

question is whether there is a justification to violate these agents' privacy to access the information. On the one hand, information owned or created by these institutions and corporations is theirs to control as much as any other private individual, and they have clear physical and social barriers and expectations that demarcate that information is off-limits to the rest of society. While, on the other hand, this protection, like all privacy protections, is not absolute and when the actions (and the information contained by the corporate entity) are harmful, there can be arguments made for the infiltration and distribution of the information. As Coleman argues, these public interest hacks are justified when the computer infiltration is used 'for the purpose of leaking documents that will have political consequence' and 'will interest the public due to the hack and the data/documents' (Coleman, 2022). The fact that an outsider shares it does not undermine the underlying ethical need.

HBGary Federal

HBGary Federal is one of the most infamous cases, not least because of the public provocations the CEO issued. HBGary Federal is a corporate firm that focused on technology security, selling technology to both the US federal government and other information assurance companies. In 2010, the CEO of HBGary Federal, Aaron Barr, publicly stated that he could use social media to track down members of Anonymous (Anderson, N., 2011). On 4 February 2011, HBGary issued the statement that, 'An international investigation into cyberactivists who attacked businesses hostile to WikiLeaks is likely to yield arrests of senior members of the group after they left clues to their real identities on Facebook and in other electronic communications, it is claimed' (Coleman, 2014: 213). The provocation was clear to the hacker collective and reinforced their hostility toward the private security industry who they regarded as 'peddling snake oil: subpar security software'. After finding a vulnerability in the HBGary Federal website Anonymous responded (Coleman, 2014: 215). This included accessing the HBGary Federal network, leaking 68,000 company emails and deleting backups (Krebs on Security, 2011), as well as 'accidentally stumbling upon a detailed PowerPoint presentation in HBGary's files entitled "The WikiLeaks Threat", a proposal for discrediting WikiLeaks and sympathetic journalists on behalf of Bank of America' (Coleman, 2014: 207).

In this HBGary case, the target is a corporate entity with a clear right to privacy regarding what they do and their internal information and communication. This privacy is well demarcated and established. There is a clear line between those on the inside and those on the outside, and they have erected significant barriers to prevent outside intrusion. Therefore, breaking into a network and accessing their information is a substantial breach of their privacy, and so would feature highly on the political violence spectrum.

However, HBGary also plays an active role in national security with the potential to directly and negatively impact people's lives if not carried out with due care. Indeed, the privatization of security more broadly, as well as the power of private corporate actors through the Internet to impact people's lives, presents them as being subject to the same expectation, ethical criteria, and therefore oversight, as state actors. Simply being a private actor does not necessarily protect you from the same ethical drivers that a political community has in keeping the power of the state in check from being applied to them. Power needs to be checked by the political community to prevent it from unjustly causing harm or damage – regardless of the actor.

The case of HBGary is an interesting one as initially there was not a significant amount of evidence that they were doing wrong. HBGary is a company that 'offers expertise in implementing intrusion detection systems and secure networking, and performs vulnerability assessment and penetration testing of systems and software' with several 'three-letter agencies, including the NSA' and Interpol who were in regular contact (Ars, 2011). In this sense they had very clearly joined the security game, and given the areas in which they were specializing – intrusion technology and surveillance – there was potential for abuse of power. In addition, leading up to the attack there was no indication of a necessary abuse of that power. HBGary did, nevertheless, actively provoke Anonymous. The CEO of a firm which claims to specialize in cyber-security publicly challenged the hacker collective, expressing their superiority in the field. Anonymous's initial response was therefore closer to a 'grey hat' hack: testing the system for weaknesses to demonstrate the lack of security of a system. At that point there could be a justification to test for weaknesses, especially given the role HBGary had in national security. However, the information that was collected by the hackers was of such a quality that it then justified a wider reveal. Looking at the information that was collected it could be argued that HBGary were an unjust threat to people's privacy and autonomy interests and so their actions were proved to be harmful and damaging. The information gained from accessing the HBGary network outlined the plan:

- Feed the fuel between the feuding groups. Disinformation. Create messages around actions to sabotage or discredit the opposing organisation. Submit fake documents and then call out the error.
- Create concern over the security of the infrastructure. Create exposure stories. If the process is believed to not be secure they are done.
- Cyber attacks against the infrastructure to get data on document submitters. This would kill the project. Since the servers are now

in Sweden and France putting a team together to get access is more straightforward.

- Media campaign to push the radical and reckless nature of wikileaks activities. Sustained pressure. Does nothing for the fanatics, but creates concern and doubt amongst moderates.
- Search for leaks. Use social media to profile and identify risky behavior of employees. (Coleman, 2014: 207)

The tactics outlined in the PowerPoint 'The WikiLeaks Threat' were 'strikingly similar to those practiced and perfected during COINTELPRO', which has been condemned for surveilling, infiltrating, discrediting and disrupting domestic American political organizations without any justification, and represented a series of ethically unjustified intelligence operations. They also 'proposed to identify and intimidate WikiLeaks donors and smear the reputation of supporters and journalists like Glenn Greenwald' (Coleman, 2014: 207). As such, Coleman argues that 'Although Anonymous did illegally compromise the servers to steal the documents, it is likely that the actions proposed in the PowerPoint presentation, had they been carried out, would have been breaking even more laws' (Coleman, 2014: 208; see also Greenwald, 2011).

In comparison, one of the most public doxxings of a politician was the attack by self-proclaimed members of Anonymous hacking then Republican vice-presidential nominee Sarah Palin's private email account and publishing some of its content (Stephey, 2008). In this case the threat is not clear. There were concerns raised that 'Palin's office refused to release hundreds of emails as part of a public records request, citing 'exemptions for deliberative process, executive privilege, attorney/client privilege, privacy, and personnel', and some suspect that Palin is using her Yahoo! account to hide info she doesn't want exposed' (Metz, 2008). However, no evidence of political abuse came forth and Palin's account was later re-hacked and re-secured by someone claiming to be 'The Good Anonymous' (Zetter, 2008). Without a clear reason to suspect abuse by Sarah Palin there is not a just cause to act, and the attack is likely to reflect more a disagreement over policy than any direct threat Palin represented to an individual or any wrongs that needed punishing. Importantly, the role of the Good Anonymous does highlight the power for hackers to correct the mistakes of their own community.

Doxxing individuals and the human flesh machine

Doxxing can also focus on an individual, releasing widely their personal details including their 'full legal names, residential addresses, unique identifiers for governmental records and services (such as social security numbers in the US), business records and documents, and personal photographs of one's self and loved ones' (Douglas, 2016: 199). The purpose can range from acting as a form of attack on the individual by revealing that which they would prefer to keep secret, to exposing wrongdoing, hoping to humiliate, cause reputational damage to someone, or promote retaliation from the wider public once their identity becomes more widely known (Solove, 2007b; Citron, 2014; Douglas, 2016). It can also vary significantly in the form it takes, how it is publicized, and who carries it out. For example, it can take on a highly intentional and organized form whereby large hacker collectives gain highly personal data that would otherwise be inaccessible and use their networks to widely distribute the information with a clear narrative on how the public should respond. But it can also take on the form of an individual collecting and circulating more publicly available information, such as a photograph of an individual in public, and spreading it across social media with the aim of gaining traction and hoping to cause some type of social statement or general social response. As Benjamin Lovelack details, these latter types of doxxing can involve 'flagging', which involves low-intensity shaming of behaviour using social media to alert users to public actions that would considered to be a breach of some, often localized, social norm, for example 'man-spreading' on public transport or parking badly. A different form can be 'investigating', where the aim is to actually name an individual through 'collective intelligence' or 'web sleuthing', where videos and documents are shared to locate an individual suspected of 'wrongdoing' with the aim of prompting social or legal repercussions once the wrongdoing has been made known (Loveluck, 2020). Though, again, what is considered to be the 'wrongdoing' can vary and can reflect various and local social norms and expectations. This type of doxxing has gained particular social traction in China, where it is referred to as the 'human flesh search engine' (人肉搜索; *Rénròu Sōusuǒ*), where through crowd sourcing, people gather together to share information, conduct investigations, and perform other actions concerning people or events of common interest (Xu and Shaoting, 2008; Cheung, 2009; Wang et al, 2010). For example, on 16 October 2010, a drunk-driving student hit a pair of university students while driving inside Hebei University, one fatally, and was reported to have shouted 'Sue me if you dare, my dad is Li Gang!' when apprehended. Following the spread of the news on Chinese Internet forums, the driver's identity was revealed as Li Qiming, the son of the deputy director of the local public security bureau. Though there were efforts to repress the story, in January 2011 Li Qiming was arrested. He was sentenced to six years in jail and ordered to pay the equivalent of $69,900 in compensation to the family of Chen Xiaofeng. Li was also ordered to pay $13,800 to the injured woman, all as the direct result of the continued pressure applied by the online citizenry (China.org.cn, 2010; Huazhong, 2010; Lam, 2010; BBC News, 2011). This type of activity is similar to what Loveluck refers to as 'hounding', where the information release 'is no longer to denounce a behaviour, to solve a puzzle or identify a suspect, but to accuse a person publicly and discredit them by providing incriminating evidence' (Loveluck, 2020). In some instances the information is shared with the police (Purshouse, 2019), while in others individuals seek to punish the targets themselves through flooding their businesses with bad reviews, unsolicited pizza deliveries, defacement of their online services or websites, or even physical destruction and harm (Loveluck, 2020).

These cases involve 'public warrants' being issued against people who have committed some perceived social *faux pas,* who are hunted in cyberspace for their personal information which is 'ruthlessly exposed and their lives mercilessly disrupted' under the 'baleful glare of publicity'. The result of such exposures have included people losing their jobs and livelihoods, suicides and murder (Cheung, 2009). What is key about these cases is that the so-called wrongdoings are often related to generally low-level social transgressions rather than the breaching of any particular law, domestic or international, nor do they often represent a significant threat to someone's vital interests. These types of operations can cause people direct harm through the violation of their privacy, autonomy and liberty as their information is used against them, as well as reputational damages that can result in further costs such as loss of livelihood, social standing, relationships and the resulting emotional distress. The impact can be devastating to those targeted and their family, and can include stalking, harassment, physical and psychological intimidation and harm, loss of reputation, financial and material costs, embarrassment and job loss (Citron, 2014). There are also additional costs to those connected to the target as they become drawn into information releases. No one is an island, and many of the negative impacts can be felt by those close to the target, whether it is family, children, friends, business colleagues or employers. These cases do not meet the threshold criteria, as those involved are not causing others significant or widespread harm, and the level of the privacy violation to those exposed is disproportional to the social ill they might have caused.

Conclusion

This chapter has argued for the important ethical value of leaking information when, firstly, it reveals wrongdoing and, secondly, when there is a right held by members of the political community to be told about information which is relevant to them fulfilling their political life. This value can in turn justify hacker intervention. Those who are acting within an organization have a duty to report wrongdoing when they become aware of it, whether they are directly involved or not, and in fact there can also be an additional duty to make sure one is aware of what is going on in one's institution. Moreover, it was argued that rather than the national security apparatus getting a free pass on this obligation, the ethical underpinning to the value national security brings to the political community places a higher expectation to reveal wrongdoing, or even to make the public aware of politically relevant information. But this should not only be restricted to state/national security actors, but private ones as well, and that when there is not an internal actor willing to fulfil this obligation then those on the outside can find a right to investigate. While this right to investigate does need some evidence to justify penetrative actions, companies that specialize in national security activity or who represent a coercive threat to the political community have actively joined the game and made themselves a legitimate target. However, targeting private individuals would rarely meet this criteria, and widespread social practices of gathering personal data and spreading it online as a form of social shaming is not justified.

5

Correcting the Failure of the State

Introduction

The previous chapters looked at the importance of people's vital interest in maintaining their autonomy, privacy and liberty, exploring how these interests manifested through various information rights, especially the freedom of speech, association and right to access relevant and important information. These chapters reflected the focus on information freedom that many hackers, especially Anonymous, have placed as a core of their political agenda. This chapter will build on these cases, expanding to look at non-cyber, non-information related threats, including when the state and its representatives fail to, first, provide and enact good laws equally and fairly, including the failure to apply fair processes, equal treatment, misapplying laws, and lacking the ability and political will to enforce the good laws; or second, when the state develops unjustifiably harmful laws, policies, procedures or institutional cultures. It will be argued that in both instances, given the failure of the state and the subsequent threat these failures represent, hackers can use political violence to defend people from harm, though the type of response must be matched to the threat posed. This chapter will look at police brutality, the failure of due and fair process, the development of laws that seek to directly discriminate and foster hatred and violence against members of the LGBTQ+ community, and the locating and unmasking of online paedophiles.

The value of good laws

Chapter 2 argued that when people come under threat there is value in any agent defending them, even if in that defence they cause the threatening agent harm. The political hacks examined here again all necessarily involve a clear coercive (or the threat of a coercive) element against a threatening agent, most often the state or its local representatives, but where the aim is to correct the misapplication of good laws or to prevent what Les Johnson referred to as 'evil laws' (Johnston, 1996). These attacks are performed outside the usual and state-sanctioned mechanisms for remedying or appealing bad state behaviour, and arguably a form of 'idealized citizenship' where the legitimacy of the political hacker's actions are determined by what the state should be doing in an idealized situation. This importantly distinguishes it from acts of private political violence that promote hatred, division and hate crimes, as they aim to protect or provide for people's vital interests. The argument is that when a state acts correctly it creates an atmosphere – made up of policies, procedures, mechanisms, cultures and actions – that protects people from unjustified harm and, at a minimum, enables people's furtherance of their own conception of the good life, and that when the state fails in this, whether from lack of will, ability or negligence, people are unjustifiably harmed. This allowance or even promotion of unjustified harm means hackers can act to defend people (Dumsday, 2009; Reynolds, 2015; for those who argue for focusing on only private individuals, see Rosenbaum and Sederberg, 1974; Little and Sheffield, 1983; Hine, 1998).

In terms of preventing evil laws, the argument is clear, as these laws, and the atmosphere they create, are instances where they unjustly threaten people's vital interests. For example, this can include punitive action that is disproportionate, unfounded, unequal, discriminatory or politically biased.[1] To make the case that a particular state activity – whether it is a law, policy, practice or culture – is necessarily harmful, the hackers need to appeal to more fundamental rights and the equal application of such rights. For example, Carl Cohen argues that certain laws can be deemed as invalid if they deprive someone from constitutionally guaranteed rights (Cohen, 1970); or what David Lefkowitz refers to as 'an undefeated moral reason' (Lefkowitz, 2007: 206); and for John Rawls whether the situation accords with 'the principles for assigning and servicing fundamental rights and liberties' (Rawls, 2009: 245). This process can be aided by appealing to universal statutes such as the Universal Declaration of Human Rights, for example, given its role in codifying these vital interests and offering international authority from which various peoples can appeal to.

However, due to the various localized interpretations of such laws and norms, these more fundamental vital interests can only act to provide a thin layer of protection. That is, there is a minimum level to which people's vital interests should be protected, but care should be given not to try to universalize higher, more complex rules and expectations. For example, the use of torture – whether physical, emotional or psychological – can be

---

[1] For justified retributive justice see Murphy, 2007: 1; Moore, 2010: 87; Berman, 2011; Duff, 2011; Markel, 2011: 50; Berman, 2013.

widely established as an unjustified form of punishment given the extreme destruction of the human condition, but more complex formulations and interpretations of localized legal norms and expectations – such as whether someone should be tried before twelve as compared to ten jurors – cannot be universally applied. In addition, for those evil laws that represent an unjustified threat to people's vital interests, depending on the nature and level of the threat the laws pose, the coercive means that can be used to defend the targets from harm can vary. The more harmful the state activity, the more harmful the hacker's attack can be in response.

On the other side of the coin, ensuring that good laws are carried out and applied fairly and equally is also about protecting people from harm. Good laws have a value in our lives as they protect, provide and create space for the fulfilment of our vital interests and their various secondary manifestations. The just application of these laws makes people's lives safer and more fulfilled (Rosenbaum and Sederberg, 1974; Shotland, 1976; Pedhazur and Perliger, 2003; Zimring, 2003; Alvarez and Bachman, 2007). These protections are often manifested through the legal frameworks and mechanisms that ensure that people are fairly and equally provided for and protected from the violence and power of each other and the state itself. When good laws are misapplied or not being enforced, or a state has failed to enact certain good laws, this can cause harm both directly to those who suffer from the failure of action, as well as promoting institutional or structural implications that cause wider harms to others. This recognizes that good laws represent a social good for all people, both reflecting and providing for people's vital interests. Failure through negligence, corruption, lack of resources, lack of political will and incompetence are therefore a threat and cause harm to individuals and society, promoting further harm to other individuals. In these instances, the good of what the state is meant to represent – a protective force, providing security for its members – can be enforced by the hackers who can 'claim to respect the law even more than the sitting government, since it takes it serious enough to want to enforce it' (Dumsday, 2009).

When good laws fail to be appropriately applied, they threaten the underlying system and in turn threaten people's lives. This is both in the abstract sense, in that the unequal application of law undermines the underlying principles that allow for the overall pursuit and protection of our vital interests, but also in a directly material sense. When good laws are unequally applied, people – mainly minorities – suffer. They lose their liberty as arrests and detainments are disproportionately applied and overly harsh; their autonomy is hindered as wider social practice forces them to internalize the discrimination and act differently from how they would have otherwise; and they face physical and mental suffering as unequal treatment emboldens social divisions, segregation and violence. Therefore, the actions of the political hackers can be justified when they act to uphold the overarching systems and structures that are valuable in people's lives, or when they act to counter or prevent the continuing threat of some actor because the state has failed to act due to a lack of ability, will or awareness, or due to corruption or negligence.

An extraordinary activity

Importantly, hacking is essentially an extraordinary response, a situation where the normal mechanisms of the state and its institutions are deemed to have failed. This means that the hacker should only respond to extraordinary situations. The political hacker is not intended to replace the state per se. Hacking should not be the norm. In an idealized situation hacking would not be needed. Therefore, the initial position is such that legitimate authority rests with the state, and that only when the state fails in delivering its ethical obligation can other actors intervene. This includes when the state is the source of the threat or when usual engagement mechanisms are redundant or could cause greater harm to those affected. Indeed if the state is unwilling or unable to prevent harm because it does not have the technical ability or manpower, then hackers can act, but they should relinquish authority once the ordinary legal justice mechanisms are available. For example, dark web activity entails a significant degree of technical skills and resources to monitor the content, but once information of harmful activity has been collected it should be forwarded for state authorities to act. If the state is unwilling to act to protect people – through a lack of political will for example – despite clear and compelling evidence of wrongdoing, then the hackers can intervene. Appealing to legal cannon on evidence and balance of probabilities can aid the hackers in knowing how and when to act.

Therefore, while such failures are arguably more apparent in states that have systematically and grievously failed due to widespread corruption, inhumane treatment, segregation and organized discrimination, hacking still occurs in states that are overall or nearly just, although simply disagreeing with the state's legitimately arrived decision is not sufficient. If, for example, the court has reviewed a case, the correct processes have been followed, and the judgment is one of not guilty, then short of new evidence, the hackers should not act. Rather, distinctions should be made between instances where the state fails because it is not infallible in an uncertain world and those where the state has acted negligently. In the case of the former, if the processes are generally sound and are not in themselves problematic, then the failure or the occasional miscarriage of justice is not sufficient to argue that the state has failed in its attempt to offer protection. If fair, consistent and appropriate action is attempted but has been 'unsuccessful' in the eyes of the hacker, the state has not failed in its attempt. Failure is different to negligence. Indeed, negligence denotes a deficiency in exercising appropriate care and judgment – whether wilful or not – that results in the harm of another. This can include both intended and unintended negligence where the actor fails to maintain the general ethical expectations of society as well as the specific additional standards of their profession.[2] Distinctions can also be made between the different parts of the state that can be held accountable. The state and its infrastructure can be sprawling and so a determination must be made to target those evidently accountable. Categorizations can therefore be made indicating where the failure is due to systematic discrimination such as racism or homophobia, corruption or failure of the duty of care, as compared to plea-bargaining, unforeseen accidents, or rules that in the majority of cases provide just results but do fail (and whose failure could not have been anticipated).

Moreover, hackers should also limit themselves to those failings that are clear, grievous, significant or widespread.[3] For example, 'rude behaviour in traffic even where there isn't an adequate police presence would not suffice to justify a vigilante response. Nor would rude behaviour on an Internet message board' (McReynolds, 2015). Given the extraordinary realm that political hacking exists in, the severity of the case should be significant. This helps avoid continuous, divergent or erratic responses from individual hackers.

In making this calculation, key critical questions can be asked regarding the level of harm caused by the hack that can then be set against the threat posed by the state's (in)action. For example, this can include accounting for the harm done to political infrastructures by the hack, ranging from confidence in the system, to financial costs when systems are damaged, to reputational costs when embarrassing information is revealed, to costs to state representatives' privacy or autonomy as private information is stolen and released, and even to costs to people's lives if critical infrastructures are shut down or hindered. In comparison, the benefits of the hack can include preventing the wider, systematic and entrenching abuse of power by the state and its representatives, acting as a mechanism to prevent bad cultures from becoming entrenched. Or, more directly, correcting the state's failure by enforcing the correct behaviour or result.

---

[2] For example, 'professional negligence' demands that individuals within a profession or position of authority are held to a higher standard where they are charged with additional duties to protect those within their care and are expected to have higher than average abilities, knowledge or training and should act diligently and knowingly (Horsey, 1994; Lepora and Goodin, 2013).

[3] These questions are similar to the 'gravity criteria' discussed at the International Criminal Court. See Ochi, 2016.

To determine if the state or its institutions and representatives have enforced good laws, it is possible to examine existing statues to give a more nuanced and detailed set of norms that the hacker can seek to maintain. The good laws themselves can act as a source of authority, providing both legitimacy and detailed local direction to the hacker. Their agreement at the local level by the political community means they are generally recognized as being worthwhile as well as specifically important in their detail. In this instance the hacker can appeal to the law of the land as it stands, and in doing so acts as the state should (McReynolds, 2015). Depending on the reason for the state failure, the type of hack can also therefore vary. For example, in those instances where the state fails due to a lack of resources in terms of technical knowledge, the hack should seek to remedy this and provide aid in that specific area. So, the hack could include gaining the previously unattainable information and then passing it on to the legitimate systems and structure for them to then operate as intended. In comparison, when the failure is due to negligence or corruption, the hack can counter those specific individuals or mechanisms that are the root cause.

Holding the police to justice: Operation BART, Ferguson and Cleveland

Operation BART came into being when San Francisco's Bay Area Rapid Transit (BART) team turned off cellphone service in reaction to a planned peaceful protest, which itself was being organized in response to the fatal shooting of Charles Hill by the police in July 2011. Even though Charles Hill was intoxicated and holding a knife, 'killing him struck many as an excessive use of force' and brought a longstanding social issue of police brutality and racism again to the forefront of society. This incident built on a previous shooting of Oscar Grant III, who 'was shot in the back while they [the police] had him pinned down' (Coleman, 2014: 304). Following the Hill shooting, a protest was organized at the Civic Centre BART station, to be followed by another protest one month later. BART blocked the cellphone reception stations to prevent the second protest. Anonymous responded by helping with the organization of the street demonstrations, defacing the BART website with an image of Guy Fawkes, attempts to bring down the BART website through distributed-denial of services (DDoS), and finally 'broke into the website belonging to the San Francisco police transport body' and then proceeded to publish 'contact details of more than 2,000 Bay Area residents, apparently stolen from this site, which was inaccessible' (Halliday, 2011). Anonymous released the statement: 'We are Anonymous, we are your citizens, we are the people, we do not tolerate oppression from any government agency. BART has proved multiple times that they have no problem exploiting and abusing the people' (Halliday, 2011). Anonymous also found a 'racy, semi–nude photo of BART's official spokesperson, Linton Johnson' and released it with the message, "'if you are going to be a dick to the public, then I'm sure you don't mind showing your dick to the public'" (Coleman, 2014: 8). A statement from BART argued that 'the interruption of mobile phone service was done Thursday to prevent what could have been a dangerous situation. It's one of the tactics we have at our disposal … And I'm not sure we would necessarily let anyone know in advance either way' (Halliday, 2011). The response from Anonymous was that 'you have not only threatened your citizens' safety, you have also performed an act of censorship. By doing this you have angered Anonymous' (CNN Wire Staff, 2011).

In a similar case, after police shot a black teenager, Michael Brown, there was a wide public outcry and demands for a suitable response from the police. The Ferguson police department initially promised to release the name of the officer who shot the 18-year-old but then did not, citing concerns for the officer's safety. Operation Ferguson followed, supporting local protests and with Anonymous seeking to apply pressure to have the police officer's name released by shutting down City Hall websites and phone services. The public messaging from Anonymous urged citizens of Ferguson to take to the streets while they caused the City's web servers to crash. Anonymous issued the statement: 'we are watching you very closely. If you abuse, harass or harm the protestors in Ferguson we will take every web-based asset of your departments and federal agencies offline' (Hunn, 2014). Anonymous activists also pasted the names and addresses of the police chief's family, and released what they claimed was the name of the police officer who killed Michael Brown. The St Louis police department released a statement on Twitter that the name released was wrong. Indeed, releasing a name did cause disagreement within the Anonymous collective, and statements on the Operation Ferguson Twitter account was issued saying that 'for the record, one last time, Operation Ferguson has NOT, repeat, NOT released the name of Mike Brown's killer, nor have we claimed to'. Indeed, Gabriella Coleman, a world-leading authority on the character and social dynamics of Anonymous, stated that 'I was surprised … Anonymous tends to care about its image quite a bit, and if they were wrong, it would be really bad' (Perlroth, 2014).

When the name failed to be released Anonymous published the St Louis police chief's personal details, including social security number and phone number (Rogers, 2014). Anonymous issued the ultimatum: 'John Belmar [the police chief], if you don't release the officer's name, we're releasing your daughter's information. You have one hour.' However, Anonymous did not follow through, and issued the statement, 'We recognize that John Belmar has had enough done to him. We will save the rest of our energy for the true perpetrator' (Perlroth, 2014).

Finally, in yet another similar case in Cleveland, Anonymous attacked the city's official website after 12-year-old Temir Rice was shot by local police, with the aim of raising awareness to the incompetence of police training and again calling for the names of the shooters (Stone, 2014). In a YouTube video, Anonymous asked the Cleveland police department to investigate and reveal the identity of the officer. After receiving mixed responses from the police department, Anonymous carried out massive DDoS attacks on the city website and took it down (Waqas, 2014).

Shutting down websites versus releasing names

Across each of these cases it can be argued that many of the hacker's actions are justified, but not all. The justification rests on whether Anonymous had sufficient reason to believe that the police as state representatives had failed in their role and that the usual mechanisms were redundant. This includes, whether the police should have responded and engaged with the concerns of the protestors and the communities affected by explicitly and publicly investigating the shootings, and specifically by releasing the names of the officers involved, and that by failing to do so had failed in an important aspect of its role, and also whether the police then had the right to prevent the protests and community action that their inaction prompted. In the BART case, the transit authority claimed that they shut down cell service for public safety reasons, attempting to prevent protest organizations from communicating and organizing via mobile devices in the face of disruptive and potentially dangerous gatherings at San Francisco underground stations. However, there is a clear right to protest and therefore for Anonymous to provide support in organizing such protests. Article 11, Freedom of Assembly and Association of the European Convention on Human Rights guarantees the right to peaceful assembly and the right to express oneself. There was no language, action or clear evidence that the protest was intended to be violent or destructive. This in turn frames the actions taken by BART as being without clear justification and runs contrary to the rights of the people. Shutting down access to communication networks as well as transportation links is a significant and disproportionate response that limited the rights of people to communicate and carry out their lives; their liberty and autonomy are both significantly limited. People's explicit political autonomy, and their ability to associate and express their socially important and timely message to both the wider community and the state itself, was directly, purposefully and significantly restrained. As a direct threat to people's autonomy the restriction limited current key forms of communication, information sharing, association organizing and expression. With this comes the damage that the loss of such communications could cause if people cannot gain access to emergency or other needed services. Critics equated such limitation of communications as akin to the blackout instituted by authoritarian governments in Egypt and Syria (Poeter, 2011).

Furthermore, the lack of unequal application of the required due process mechanisms in a timely and public fashion represents an important problem because such rules are a form of localized oversight over the power of the state's ability to use violence against its own political community. Across all three cases there were significant delays, refusal to engage and publish information, or carry out a public demonstration of oversight processes. Given the public responses to the shootings, credence can be given to concerns that public naming of the officers could prompt violent backlashes, and this should be taken very seriously. But there was a lack of dialogue, engagement and some form of public oversight procedure, highlighting a lack of willingness to engage with the public in a key area of concern and with no counterbalance to the state's power to use violence. Indeed, the police departments mishandled the incidents across all cases. Public statements, reassurances, investigations and inclusion of the local communities were essentially the demands of the protesters and hackers alike. The response from the police was to shut themselves off, close ranks and escalate the confrontation in the case of BART.

For the DDoS attacks specifically, the aim of the attacks was both to raise wider awareness of the situation as well as acting as a pressure on authorities to act in accordance with what the hackers and protesters thought was needed, which was some form of public oversight. The DDoS attacks were targeted against those involved while only impacting non-critical systems. These are part of the direct infrastructure that was involved in the removal of people's right to associate and communicate, yet the information contained in that system was not directly vital, so that its temporary loss would not put people in harm's way or unable to access emergency help. The threshold of need is also arguably reached. In all three cases, there is a clear, political event going on that the wider political community is concerned about and involves the accusation of an unjustified police shooting of innocents. This is an important event to society as a whole and the reaction by the state is of direct political importance in determining if it is applying its own good laws fairly and equally.

However, when the attacks turn to revealing personal information, the justification fails. The hackers exposed the identities of BART customers, meaning that those who were not involved were being affected. The personal information of these customers is theirs to own and determine who has access to it; the hacker's information dump undermines their vital interest in privacy. Even the doctrine of double effect cannot help as the harm was a necessary part of the operation; a foreseen and intended consequence as the harm was designed to embarrass BART. This means that the harm to them is unjustified, poisoning the hack. However, Anonymous did release a statement on Twitter claiming that the release of personal information was not authorized by the collective: 'No one claimed responsibility for the hack. Some random Joe joined a channel and released the data to the press … The leak today of BART officer data could be the work sanctioned by those who truly support Anonymous, or agent provocateurs. Stay skeptical' (Jackson, 2011). In addition, one area Anonymous is often concerned with is actual data security, and when it published the details of BART members, one thing it said was that 'We apologize to any citizen that has his information published, but you should go to BART and ask them why your information wasn't secure with them' (Olson, 2011). So the release of names is not justified. However, the weaknesses of BART's security over its own information is also ethically important, and highlighting these weaknesses (while not revealing people's identities) can be justified.

It should be noted, however, that by releasing names of someone in a highly politically charged and divisive event – a name that would otherwise be relatively difficult to know otherwise – the hackers place themselves directly in the chain of causation for what happens to that individual. By doing so, they place themselves as an instigator of the harm that could then befall the officer as a result of the release, and so they create a relationship, and a duty of care, to that individual (*Donoghue v Stevenson*, 1932). This means that any harm that then transpires is their responsibility. If the release of a name and address results in a non-Anonymous mob attacking that individual and that this response was reasonably foreseeable – which given the politically charged nature of the situation is likely – then the hackers face a significant degree of blame for any harm suffered, as much as if they were physically part of the attacking mob. Equally, if they release information that then results in other harms or damages – psychological, reputational or financial for example – if such responses were reasonably foreseeable, they again face a significant part of the blame for that harm. This places an important responsibility on the political hackers to be aware of the implications of their actions and to share the information with the right audiences in the right ways.

Nigeria/Uganda

In Nigeria and Uganda, Anonymous launched hacking attacks in response to their anti-LGBTQ+ legislation, taking down government websites in response to the 'intent to pass a law that would jail LGBT people for up to 14 years' along with other discriminatory policies. Anonymous declared, 'Nobody should live in fear of being jailed, when their only action is loving another consenting adult, regardless of gender … Failure to follow our order will unleash a torrent of fury aimed directly at the direction of your administration, starting with some startling but unsurprising evidence of corruption in your ranks' (Ford, 2012; Littauer, 2013).

In these cases it can be argued that given the political and social climate that members of the LGBTQ+ community have suffered (including those wishing to act on their behalf), there is a clear threat to their physical, emotional and psychological interests. Examples of the violent and public abuse of homosexuals, including by official authorities such as the police, serve to highlight the social problems and the harm that LGBTQ+ individuals are likely to face as a result of a law that encourages discrimination and the normalization of existing abusive treatment. Furthermore, social stigmatization and institutional abuse are likely to limit individuals coming forward, restricting ordinary legal avenues. The state represents the source of the threat and so calls out for a new entity to act on behalf of those who would be harmed, and given the threat to the lives of LGBTQ+ individuals in Uganda and Nigeria, using hacks that cause a minimal amount of physical damage in order to raise awareness of the problem to the wider public and to put pressure – even blackmail – on the government is justified as it seeks to prevent harms and defend others against clear physical and social harms. While shutting down government websites might negatively impact people, the damage caused is less than a legislation that encourages and fosters severe harm to a portion of society, especially when the websites concerned are predominately for information of low importance and the action does not prevent access to critical services. These cases represent an instance of the state erecting bad laws that unjustly discriminate a portion of their community while also fostering and promoting a homophobic atmosphere that will cause harm to the LGBTQ+ community. Therefore, given the minimum harm caused by the attack, and the potential harm caused by the introduction of such laws, the act is justified and proportional – and arguably could even justify more forceful interventions if it could prevent the harms being suffered by LGBTQ+ individuals in these countries. This could include widespread and significant shutdown of non-emergency government systems, costly damage to cyber-systems, and penetrative investigations into government behaviour for other wrongdoing.

Stopping dark-web paedophiles

One notable set of cases includes locating and revealing the identities of online paedophiles. Through Operation Darknet, 2011, Operation DeathEaters, 2015, and Operation Darknet Relaunch, 2017, Anonymous sought to collect evidence against international paedophiles rings so as to 'bring them to justice'. Anonymous reported that 'The Westminster paedophile ring is one of many cases where Operation DeathEaters has actively pursued and sought truth, in order to end the hideous crimes concealed behind the British elite' (Eleftheriou-Smith, 2015). In this case it can be argued that the laws had been broken, causing a significantly high degree of harm to people. Individuals – children who are unable to give consent – were being directly harmed physically, mentally and emotionally through the creation of pornographic material and those who share or utilize it but do not necessarily create it are still complicit in the harm being done by placing themselves as a contributing and encouraging factor (Kutz, 2007: 294). This harm means that there is a duty for an intervention to prevent it. The actual damage done by the hackers themselves is limited, even though they were actively violating people's privacy in a sphere especially designed to re-emphasize privacy, the benefit brought by the hack greatly outweighs this. Moreover, the hackers then passed on the information collected to the authorities for them to carry out the necessary examination and application of state-retributive justice. The hackers only revealed the identity of those involved, rather than carrying out sweeping collection methods to reveal everyone who used the dark web. Furthermore, given the nature of the dark web, the ability of the state to locate such threats is limited and so aid from the hacker community supports the state's attempts at stopping such activity. In this instance, therefore, the hacker's actions were justified.

Fighting ISIS

After the terrorist attack in Paris 2015 against the newspaper *Charlie Hebdo*, which killed 12 and injured 11 others, Anonymous devoted itself to locating and rooting out the social media accounts of ISIS supporters. It's efforts were subsequently ramped up following the ISIS Paris attacks on 13 November 2015, when Anonymous stated that it was 'at war' with ISIS: 'you, the vermin who kill innocent victims, we will hunt you down like we did those who carried out the attacks on Charlie Hebdo'; 'we as a collective will bring an end to your reign of terror. We will no longer turn a blind eye to your cruel and inhumane acts of terrorism towards all others … THIS WILL NOT BE TOLERATED ANY LONGER. ISIS … the war is on' (Hern, 2015). A loosely related group, BinarySec, also confirmed it would start acting against ISIS in cyberspace. For more than a year the hacker collective waged an online war against ISIS and its varied supporters. During this time Anonymous has claimed 'to have dismantled some 149 Islamic State-linked websites and flagged roughly 101,000 Twitter accounts and 5,900 propaganda videos' (Brooking, 2015). One of the most iconic hacks has included the hacker WauchulaGhost, who in remembrance for the murder of 49 people at the gay Orlando nightclub defaced ISIS's Twitter accounts to make them 'as fabulously gay as humanly possible', as well as revealing IP addresses, phone numbers and other contact information for fellow hackers to use (Hern, 2016).

ISIS embodies a modern, cyber-reliant terrorist group that uses the Internet for communication, recruitment, ideology sharing and radicalization, marking the attacks by Anonymous as significant acts against ISIS's efforts (Gerwehr and Daly, 2006: 83; Denning, 2010; Sachan, 2012; *Public Prosecutor v Hicheur*, 2012: 9). ISIS's Twitter and social media activities have played a direct role in its recruitment propaganda machine and are an integral part of its terrorist agenda. The hacker's objective is to collect intelligence on ISIS membership and activities as well as undermining its recruitment abilities. Therefore, the justification is easy to establish as ISIS represented a close, real and direct threat. It has publicly kidnapped and killed people, recruited and promoted terrorist attacks, and engaged in a sustained and unjustified war. Furthermore, in the proportionality calculation, given the limited and directed harm caused by Anonymous in comparison to the harm caused by ISIS, the gains outweigh the costs. Anonymous flagged publicly available Twitter feeds and video data, and while it defaced private websites the damage was minimal, only directed at those connected to the terrorist organization, and outbalanced in comparison the harm caused by ISIS. Recruitment online for terrorist organizations like ISIS is often difficult to locate and control, especially given the limited expertise and resources of the state, and Anonymous did pass the collected information to legal authorities for further action.

Conclusion

This chapter explored the expanding political hacker's mandate, as they engage in ever-widening circles of political activism. Despite the often-quoted criticism that political hackers are 'taking justice into their own hands', this is not necessarily the case. While it might feel like the hackers are punishing wrongdoers, they are in fact still working to provide defence of others. There is still the coercive element seen in the other chapters, but it is still not for punishing, but rather it is to either remedy the wrong being perpetuated directly or to force state actors to correct their actions and remedy the harm.

6

Looking Back, Moving Forward

Introduction

As outlined in the Introduction, it is not the aim of the ethical framework to inadvertently open the door to all private forms of political violence, nor is it to justify all hacking; the purpose is to highlight the space for hackers to operate as legitimate actors and to guide hacker activity by detailing what actions are justified toward what end. Following the detailing of the ethical framework in Chapters 1 and 2, and the application in Chapters 3, 4 and 5, there are two further tasks. One is to establish some critical mechanisms – both theoretical and practical – to stop abuse and to aid hackers in reaching ethically justified decisions. The second is to widen the perspective to examine what implications this work has on how society should respond and reconceptualize political hacking. This includes a reflection on how existing legal and social frameworks are reacting to political hacking most broadly in order to highlight how they can better reflect the central argument for an (un)ethical hacker, a reconceptualization of 'security', and the argument for a more open and engaged set of state actors.

Limiting the abuse

Right intention

One of the key challenges with an ethical framework like the one outlined in this book is the potential for abuse. This can include using the ethical framework to justify one's actions by meeting the criteria superficially in a check-list approach, resulting in unjustified harm or personal gain masquerading as an ethical benefit. Such abuse is an established challenge for all ethical frameworks, especially those that argue for the justification of defensive harm or are seen to work in a 'box-ticking' manner. In limiting this potential for abuse it is essential to stress and reflect on both the theoretical underpinning of the ethical framework itself in order to avoid abuse through superficial engagement, as well as some of the practical mechanisms that can be entrenched to aid in a fuller and correct critical reflection and engagement with the theoretical principles. As Candice Delmas argues, such reflective constraints are necessary and useful as they help distinguish between 'the Ku Klux Klan's vigilante terrorism and self-defence ... of the Deacons Defence ... or between British feminist street artist Bambi's politically conscious graffiti and swastika vandalism' (Delmas, 2018b: 48).

At the core of this book has been the argument that political hacking is justified when it prevents harm; and so operations are not justified when there is no threat to a third party's fundamental vital interests. This is itself a limit on those hacks that are for personal gain of some form. Fundamental to ensuring this is emphasizing the role of 'intention'. That is, it is not enough to have an objective justification by acting in defence of some existing threat, but one must also possess a proper subjective intention to act in line with the underlying justification. This involves, first, recognizing that the principles are not simply listed criteria, but are reflective of deeper ethical arguments. These deeper arguments allow for an adaptation to other examples as new techniques or unpredictable operations occur, as well as emphasizing the need to reflect on their foundational principles. Secondly, that the intention behind an act alters the moral quality of the act. Intention has become an essential part of our common moral discourse: how we talk about, speculate on, and judge actions, which is reflected in the significant role it plays in judicial systems the world over (Thomson, 1986: 101–2; Scanlon and Dancy, 2000). Indeed, Western law makes the distinction between *actus reus*, 'guilty act', and *mens rae*, 'guilty mind', whereby a judge will often consider the perpetrator's intention in deciding how 'guilty' someone is and the sentence they should have. There is a legal and moral distinction between murder and manslaughter in that we distinguish between a premeditated crime and one that was accidental or was never intended (Orend, 2006: 46). In politics, leaders must be able to justify their decisions, noting that they had the right intentions: 'for those that slip the dogs of war, it is not sufficient that things turn out for the best' (Lackey, 1989: 32). This is why the principle of right intention features strongly within defensive frameworks as the intentions of an actor can alter how we judge them.[1] Indeed, traditionally the principle of right intention was stated as being necessary so that the 'belligerents should have a rightful intention, so that they intend the advancement of good or the avoidance of evil'. Early just war theorist, St Thomas Aquinas was clear to stress that the right intention should be for the common good of both parties – for the wicked and righteous alike. This was because it is possible

---

[1] Mona Fixdall and Dan Smith argue that the intervention in Rwanda in 1994 was of a lesser moral quality because it was seen to be motivated by a desire to play the great power game in Africa (Fixdall and Smith, 1998: 300).

for 'war to be declared by legitimate authority and just cause, yet nonetheless be made unlawful through a wicked intention' (Aquinas, 2002: 214). This prevents an actor from carrying out actions of lust, greed or domination even if there is a clear threat. The principle of right intention ensures that the justification put forward is accurate and true and not a disguise for ulterior motives. As Delmas notes, 'Of course resistors always act for the sake of some interests – the question is what kind of interests they pursue (Are they basic human interests or special interests of privileged groups?)' (Delmas, 2018b: 49).

A clear challenge to this is that understanding a single actor's true intentions is never easy, and it becomes particularly difficult for hacking, given the diverse and anonymous nature of the actors involved. However, 'intentions are neither infinitely indescribable nor irreducible private and mysterious' (Orend, 2006: 47). Rather, the intentions are a reflection of the operation itself. Indeed, in common moral discourse it is argued that the central intention or justification of an action should be reflected in the means used, targets chosen and outcomes pursued (Thomson, 1986: 101– 2; Lackey, 1989: 32; Scanlon and Dancy, 2000). For example, if the justification is one of self-defence, then the actions must flow directly from this and not involve tactics of domination or subjugation of the aggressor. We can track back from the methods and circumstances of a situation to understand the intention. There is an important interconnectedness here: at their core, intentions are a manifestation of the justifications put forward, and the means employed to secure that justification are a reflection of that intention.

This will, therefore, both place limits on the means used as well creating an opportunity to examine the key features of a hack – the techniques used, the position/role/function of those targeted, the normative narrative delivered, and what types of harms are allowed – to map out and evaluate the operation. To achieve this mapping each part of the political hack – the political agenda, methods, targets, narratives and ends of the operation – are examined, both as individual parts as well as how they (in)congruently map to each other to create the operation as a whole. All have a part to play in how we judge an action, and all are interrelated to each other. Therefore, the whole enterprise must map accurately across the hacking operation: what method is chosen, who the targeted is, the rhetoric employed, the amount of damage or harm allowed, and the limits they place on themselves.

As the justification is one of self-defence, then the operation's intention must flow directly from this and the actions must be related to the threat. The intention should be to defend against *this* threat. This intention will then be reflected in the operation that is then carried out. This means that those hacking operations for economic gain or personal fame are not justified and that this intention would be apparent because the methods used would be inappropriate for the superficially stated political objective.

In addition to this right intention, the hack should be considered as a last resort. That is, political hacking is not and should not be the norm; it is an extraordinary response to a significant failure. Therefore, it should be both proportional to the threat posed as well as only resorted to when other, less harmful, activities are redundant. This way, if it is possible, more harmful acts are avoided. However, as Robert Phillips warns, 'it is a mistake to suppose that "last" necessarily designates the final move in a chronological series of actions' (Phillips, 1984: 14). If it did, then force would never be legitimized since one could always continue to flounder in the system with the illusion of progressing while little actual change is achieved. Rather, it demands that actors 'carefully evaluate all the different strategies that might bring about the desired end, selecting force as it appears to be the only feasible strategy for securing those ends' (Bellamy, 2006: 123). If time and circumstances permit other means short of force, they should be used. But there is not a rigid set of steps that one must follow at all times, beginning with the least harmful and ending in political violence.

Practical limits

While it was argued in Chapter 2 that the ethical drive to protect people from harm was more important than the need to wait around for some official actor to intervene, there are some ethically relevant processes that can aid in ensuring that the correct target is subjected to the appropriate type and level of response. Indeed, there are some key virtues found within a deliberative democracy that can help stress some useful principles going forward. At the heart of this is the importance of allowing for critique, debate and reflection. This is important because personal bias is a significant problem. Individuals are the worst judge in their own courts. A deliberative process provides the opportunity for people's conceptions and perceptions to be challenged in order to achieve a greater understanding of events. As Simone Chambers argues, 'all theories of deliberative democracy contain something that could be called a publicity principle' whereby the 'salutary effects of going public with the reasons and arguments backing up a policy, proposal or claim' can 'expose injustice, corruption and general dirty deals that might otherwise go unnoticed' (Chambers, 2004: 390). However, while Chambers does note the 'considerable disagreement' over putting this into practice, the importance of being able to convey the reasoning in terms of public goods over private reason is clear. Moreover, Chambers argues that such an ethos can even be replicated in secretive environments by still 'applying the publicity test by welcoming diversity of opinion' (Chambers, 2004: 408). This presents two aspects: first that there is an inherent value in allowing a plurality of voices to engage, and second, that in secretive environments, and even with a limited number of contributions, one must imagine defending the action publicly.

So, while it is not the aim here to give strict organizational specifics, it is still possible to highlight underlying principles. This would include, firstly, a deliberation process to allow critique, debate and reflection to minimize the likelihood of incorrect activity. Hacker intentions, objectives and demands should be given the opportunity for others to reflect on their reasoning and provide input. This could include a means for publicly debating these objectives and intentions as needed, so that they can be sufficiently interrogated and determined if they are sound. This could be supported by a means of collecting and sharing different opinions and giving individuals the opportunity to voice objections, offer support or provide new information. Part of this is the argument 'that if each member of a jury has an equal and independent chance better than random, but worse than perfect, of making a correct judgment, then the probability of a correct majority judgment increases by having more jurors' (List, Elsholtz and Seeley, 2009: 755; also Grofman et al, 1983; List and Goodin, 2001). This does not mean that juries are always the correct answer. Indeed, *Condorcet's paradox* is the observation that majority preferences can be 'irrational' (specifically, intransitive) even when individual preferences are 'rational'. This can be a problem when psychological influences – social prejudices and racisms, mob mentality and witch-hunts – significantly distort the reflective processes. But what is important is that deliberative processes can be aided by offering a means of reflecting and interrogating the beliefs of the hackers and can aid in minimizing any personal biases. There is also a greater chance that the claim will represent the ideas of the wider population if more people are involved in the decision-making process.

However, given that the mechanisms might vary across different hackers, what is more important is the embodied mentality. That is, to be able to 'defend one's policy preferences in public' so that the decision 'leans one towards using public reason' or 'reasons that this public at large could accept'. Such a principle 'encourages participants to examine their own beliefs and arguments', promoting critical self-reflection within decision-makers, while also conferring legitimacy as the policy 'ought be to in the general interest' (Chambers, 2004: 390). The mindset and critical question should be whether if one was to have to defend oneself in a public court, could it be defended.

In reflecting across the cases discussed, where there were significant problems, it often involved a lack of wider engagement with the hacking community. For example, in the Sarah Palin case where the emails were accessed and released without reviewing whether there was evidence within the emails to justify the wider release, Anonymous denounced the actions as a lone individual acting without discussion with the collective, which then prompted an effort to resecure the emails by the 'Good Anonymous'. In the BART case, where personal details were released, Anonymous explicitly stated that 'Some random Joe joined a channel and released' the information without authorization (Jackson, 2011). While these might be excuses, and there is not a specific number of people required to make something justified, and it does not mean one person cannot act justly, what this reflects is the value of critical reflection and the power that multiple forms of input can provide.

For some, these mechanisms might appear antithetical to hackers, especially given the portrayal of the lone-wolf teenage malcontent sitting in a room alone expressing their angst, but many hackers are part of a group, community or collective. Indeed, Anonymous prides itself on being a leaderless, open and fluid organization with a strong insistence on anonymity, but in practice still manages to operate like a super-organism, whereby individuals coalesce around a particular cause and cooperate to produce the necessary results. Coleman has detailed at length the internal conversations, debates, reconciliations and deliberations that hackers carry out as they process the available information and prepare for an operation. The processes and management of groups like Anonymous are 'not formalised, much less codified' and rely on 'rough consensuses and running code' similar in methodology to the 'occupy movement' whereby individuals came together to fulfil a particular goal but move away again once the movement is over (Serracino-Inglott, 2013). However, there is value in having internal decisions that are typified by horizontality and consensus. This approach promotes plurality of opinion and a reliance on mass contribution, which limits bias and interrogates evidence, though this should be encouraged through explicit, public and open dialogue on online public forums with an established decision-making process. For example, using platforms for sharing ideas that then collectively rate those ideas can act as a useful means of generating a communal understanding of a topic from a diverse global membership. Most notable among these is reddit.com, social news aggregation, web content rating, and discussion websites where members submit content – such as links, text posts and images – that are then voted up or down by other members.[2] Anonymity can still be maintained and it can reflect an anti-hierarchical ethos, though making it more officially open to outside involvement and formalized to ensure alternative points of view.

Indeed, this is something some collectives have already become acutely aware of as large collectives such as Anonymous have developed a strong brand identity that they have increasingly cultivated, and internally policed, despite being comprised of a loosely connected set of individuals. The 'collective consciousness' acts as a hive mind, as both an amalgamation of the shared beliefs as well as a means of moderating the lone actors. As such,

---

[2] See https://www.redditinc.com

we can view these collectives as free-flowing groupings, sometimes forming around specific issues or even being motivated around operational ability, but still professing a clear political rhetoric that the collective in that instance is using to define its ethical ends.

Political hacking and reshaping the approach

Political and legal responses

Moving forward, one of the biggest challenges is the way political hacking is conceived and approached through the existing political and criminal justice systems. Part of this is that political hacking is conceptualized as a significant threat, both broadly to society's stability as well as in terms of the specific costs it represents. In purely financial costs, various reports place hacking costing 'the US economy $100 billion in economic damages and 500,000 lost jobs every year' (McAfee and the Center for Strategic and International Studies, 2013). While the political and social framing by politicians and media is encompassing and ill-defined for what is an incredibly nuanced, diverse and fluid phenomenon, portraying all hackers as 'lonely malicious criminals' and with no real nuance between those hacking for financial benefit, thrills, reputation, chaos or beneficial political ends (Thomas, 2002: 6). Nor is there a real distinction between those attacks which would cause wide significant, systematic damage to people or property, or more localized attacks with temporary, transitory or limited impact.

Even when there is a focus on political hacking as something distinct, political elites across all branches of government have an explicitly extreme conceptualization that places this type of hacking as closer to the cyber-terrorist category than social progressive. This perception reflects a high-level fear of the potential threat hackers could represent, whereby the extreme possibilities are then applied to all cases regardless of the event, damages caused, or political activity engaged in. The fear of the possibility of hackers taking over and crashing a plane or shutting down the electric grid are experienced at the highest level of government and plays a significant role in the framing of all hacking regardless of methods or ends. Indeed, General Keith Alexander, while serving as Director of the National Security Agency (NSA) in 2012, informed the White House that within a year or two Anonymous would have the power to bring about power outages through cyber-attacks (Gorman, 2012; Bamford, 2013). This fear is then exacerbated by the inherent nature of political hacking: that is it secretive, acting outside the state's usual structures and control, with wide-reaching but unknown abilities that are matched by the lack of technical understanding by outsiders as to what political hackers can and want to do. However, this heightened fear reflects Cass Sunstein's work on the current growth of a 'risk culture' where threats are distorted and overemphasized in their importance, promoting fear and social decohesion within society while driving an escalation of security policy (Sunstein, 2005). The result has been an aggressive approach to locating and punishing political hackers through the criminal justice system.

The reaction to political hacking is problematic as it shows both an excessively aggressive legal response, while also further reflecting and entrenching the existing power asymmetries within society, limiting the opportunity for political hacking to exert its socially reforming power. That is, hacking is both a product of the lack of true political engagement opportunities, as well as being a remedy that is actively being restricted. As Coleman argues, the current system inherently acts to restrain hacking as a legitimate form of political engagement as 'corporate actors not only can continue to voice their positions just fine through multiple channels, but can also … put defendants through costly time-consuming legal processes' (Coleman, 2014). However, rather than being a threat to social stability, political hacking can represent a mechanism for a better, more inclusive society. As Celikates argues:

> far from posing a danger to democracy, various forms of political contestation … can be seen as vital to reinvigorating what is left of the anarchic political energies of the public sphere and pushing or encouraging institutions to pay more attention to the points of view and demands articulated by the greater variety of more or less organised actors in the public sphere. (Celikates, 2015: 163)

The value of such contestation can include 'reopening deliberation … enlarged deliberation and representation … dissemination of viewpoints, information and arguments … stimulating the imagination of alternative possibilities … pushing for actions, decisions and outcomes where institutions suffer political inertia' (Celikates, 2015: 166). The development of digital tools 'massively expands the repertoire of contention' from some of the more passive forms such as 'blogs, bulletin boards, and online petitions' to the ones which necessarily utilize more destructive actions such as distributed-denial of services (DDoS) attacks and virtual sit-ins (Celikates, 2015: 167).

One of the most revealing cases of this political-legal reaction is that of Aaron Swartz who faced multiple felony charges, up to $1 million in fines and 35 years in prison, before tragically taking his own life. Swartz was arrested for downloading a cache of academic journals from JSTOR through his access to the MIT network while a research fellow. Aaron Swartz had a JSTOR account that allowed him access for his research work, and he used that access to download articles in bulk over a period of several weeks. On 6 January 2011, Swartz was arrested on two state charges of breaking and entering with intent to commit a felony. By July he was facing a series of felony indictments under the Computer Fraud and Abuse Act (CFAA) that was pursued with an aggressive prosecution, with up $1 million in fines and 35 years in prison, which ultimately resulted in Aaron committing suicide. Coleman argues that as part of the aggressive legal pursuit the 'main prosecutor, Stephen Heymann, nevertheless had the audacity to compare the Internet pioneer to a rapist and suggested he had systematically revictimized MIT'. Coleman goes on to argue that the 'downloading of academic articles, many of them researched and written by tax dollars, was wholly undeserving of a 35-year sentence and a felony charge' (Coleman, 2014: 172). On 6 January 2013, Swartz took his own life. Anonymous responded: 'Two weeks ago today, a line was crossed. Two weeks ago today, Aaron Swartz was killed. Killed because he was forced into playing a game he could not win – a twisted and distorted perversion of justice – a game where the only winning move was not to play' (Coleman, 2014: 368).

Comparing the legal response of cases like those against Aaron Swartz and Anonymous to similar non-cyber variations it is clear that there is a fundamentally different mentality and approach to the pursuing and punishing of political hackers: 'given what transpires during a DDoS attack, and whatever one might think of the risks and seriousness of it, one thing seems certain: those charges levelled against Anonymous participants in the US and UK tend to be out of line' with a clearer set of 'harsher punishments' for the online actions in comparison to similar offline equivalences (Coleman, 2014: 140). For example, if physical impact is taken as the benchmark, then when it is compared to similar levels of physical attacks, it would mean that many political hacks should be treated as misdemeanour offense, with a possible penalty of up to 30 days jail time, and not the current practice of labelling them as felonies with the significantly higher amount of jail time and/or fine (Higgins, 2013). For example, the protests by Extinction Rebellion that caused physical damages totalling around £6,000 and Delta 5's obstruction of oil transport were considered to be misdemeanours rather than federal crimes, which significantly limited and reduced the punishment delivered (Wong, 2016; BBC News, 2019).

Part of the problem is that existing laws are outdated compared to current technology and society's use of that technology. In this space the most utilized laws include the Computer Fraud and Abuse Act (CFAA) in the US, originally passed in 1896 with updates in 1984 and 2000; the Computer Misuse Act 1990 (CMA) in the UK; and the Council of Europe's Convention on Cybercrime, which includes looking at cyber-attacks that cross jurisdictional boundaries. Taking the CFAA as a key example, it is arguably vague and overly encompassing in both its framing and use. The CFAA imposes both criminal and civil liabilities on unauthorized access to damage a protected computer. It has been significantly noted that both the legal text and application are broad, unreflective and inappropriate. As

Scheuerman argues, the open-endedness of the CFAA's 'fraud' and 'abuse' is idiosyncratic and 'probably unrecognisable to most ordinary people' and that, 'Revealingly, the statutes in question predate the emergency and mass availability of the Internet' and is essentially 'obsolete given the startling innovations' (Scheuerman, 2016: 304). Indeed, Coleman argues that the CFAA is 'a decidedly blunt legal instrument – so broad that it offers prosecutors tremendous power in any legal proceedings that relates, in virtually any way – to the vague notion of "unauthorised computer access"' and that the 'activities need not be "hacking" at all' (Coleman, 2014: 24).

The aim here is not necessarily a legal one. There are various critiques of the CFAA that argue that there is significant legal ambiguity over what counts as a 'computer', when legitimate access is 'exceeded' and what it means to act without proper 'authorization' (especially for those, like whistleblowers, who operate from within an organization who do have authorization) (Tuma, 2011). Rather, the point is that the use of such laws and the social response is indicative of the broader problem. When the CFAA was first proposed in 1986 the main concern was preventing damage to governmental computerized systems or large financial institutions that would result in significant and widespread damage to economic markets, or nuclear control systems (Hendler, 2013). This type and level of fear has continued unabated with doomsday scenarios featuring in popular culture and the public psyche and still dominates how the law is applied. However, the use of computers has diversified significantly and the costs suffered for losses are equally diverse. In *United States* v *Kramer*, the courts quoted Steve Wozniak, co-founder of Apple Computer Co, stating that 'everything has a computer in it nowadays', expanding the potential realm of interest for the CFAA. In doing so, this increases the diverse range of computer systems employed throughout society, which equally expands the levels of impact technology can have on people's lives, including much lower or temporary impacts. This creates a vast range of points of impact for a hacker, with a correspondingly large range of impacts that hackers can have on people, both high and low. This means there needs to be more nuance in terms of better understanding exactly what impact is suffered.

Moreover, the interpretation of costs is overly expansive, especially in civil terms, as the CFAA allows for civil reparation claims to be made against the hackers. For example, it can include the cost of hiring consultants to investigate a hack, even if there are no damages caused; the cost of subsequent security enhancements to the system, which should have originally been the responsibility of the system's owner and ultimately their own failure; and a predicted cost of loss of earnings for a website shutdown, which in one case was estimated at $1,000,000 for a loss of 1 hour of service time. Indeed, the civil clause allows for significant costs to put on individuals: 'Any person who suffers damage or loss by reason of a violation of this section may maintain a civil action against the violator to obtain compensatory damages and injunctive relief or other equitable relief' (18 USC § 1030(g)). This became of particular significance when 'a 38 year old truck driver, Eric J Rosol, was fined for running an automated DDoS tool against Koch Industries website for 60 seconds', and though the 'actual financial costs were less than $15,000' he was 'slapped with a fine of $183,000 – even though a far worse physical crime, arson, would earn a fine of only $6,400 in the same state' (Coleman, 2014: 140–1). The civil clause of the CFAA allowed Koch Industries to claim for the cost of hiring a consultancy firm for advice on mitigating the attack. The civil clause should therefore include a more specific intent to cause harm.

A final update to the political-legal approach to political hacking should include advancements in the defence available, where again intention can play an important role. That is, when it is not the intention of the hackers to cause harm for the sake of personal gain or the simple enjoyment of causing destruction, but the intention is to protect people from harm, then this intention and related context needs to be considered. Indeed, killing someone can differ in how it is judged depending on whether it was intentional (murder), unintentional (manslaughter, negligence) or in self-defence (justified). Self-defence is available as a legal defence to crimes committed using force. Indeed, many of the legal tests used for self-defence are reflected in the previously outlined criteria. For example, in the UK the basic principles of self-defence are set out in *Palmer* v *R* [1971] AC 814 (approved in *R* v *McInnes*, 55 Cr App R 551), and includes the principle of necessity: 'It is both good law and good sense that a man who is attacked may defend himself. It is both good law and good sense that he may do, but only do, what is reasonably necessary'. This principle of necessity is detailed in section 3 of the Criminal Law Act 1967 as: 'A person may use such force as is reasonable in the circumstances in the prevention of crime, or in effecting or assisting in the lawful arrest of offenders or suspected offenders or of persons unlawfully at large' (Criminal Law Act 1967, §3(1)). This means asking whether someone faced a relevant threat to themselves or someone else with no one present to defend them, making the intervention necessary. In making this assessment, two further questions can be asked: first, was the use of force necessary in the circumstances? And, second, was the force used reasonable in the circumstances? For the first criteria, it has been argued that the purpose of political hacking is to replicate the value of the state and would, in ideal circumstances, not be needed. It should not be the first port of call, but represents an instance where the usual mechanisms have failed or are redundant. For the second, it again raises the issue of proportionality in terms of whether the harm caused by the hack was reasonable, given the threat and options available. Also, and importantly, there is no rule in law to say that a person must wait to be struck first before they may defend themselves (see R v *Deana*, 2 Cr App R 75).

Part of this includes a need to update the legal conceptualization of self-defence, as traditionally it is used to justify severe (deadly) force when one's own life is (feared to be) under threat. As discussed in Chapter 2, those scenarios presented when exploring the issue of self-defence often include a clear, direct threat to one's life that then justifies responding with similar force to prevent it. Political hacking, on the other hand, causes a much lower level of force and so also only needs a suitably lower level of threat to justify it. As argued in Chapter 1 and Chapter 2, there is a direct link between the level of violence caused by the hack and the level of threat it is defending against.

The adjustment needed, therefore, is to enable a defence that takes into account the degree of impact with greater nuance, understanding more precisely what is being targeted, the threat that this target represents, and the opportunity for a self-defence legal defence that includes providing for or protecting people's vital interests. What this means for prosecution under legal frameworks such as the CFAA is that the case is not just determining whether the individual accused is involved, or the degree of their involvement, but also whether they can claim that the damage they caused was protecting someone from harm, whether it was proportional and reasonably appropriate, given other options available, and whether it was directed at those who were the cause of the threat. This should shape how the state views and seeks out hackers.

Conceptualization of national security

Another important consequence of this work is the need to redefine what is meant by security, especially in terms of national security, one that moves away from it being seen as in opposition to people's fundamental rights, and more as the means of providing protection for an individual's core human rights. This is key in terms of understanding what counts as a threat and how people can therefore respond. At the centre of a narrow conceptualization of security is the prioritization of securing our physical form from damage, pain or death, which has been extrapolated over time to equate national security with protecting the state and 'the prevention of or resilience against deliberate attack' (Schneier, 2006: 12). It can be argued, however, that the value of security, and therefore the right or expectation to have security, is directly linked to the value that individuals have in maintaining their vital interests. That is, security is the condition by which one's vital interests are maintained and protected, and so should be seen as the processes and protections designed to maintain all of a person's vital interests in their physical and mental integrity, autonomy, liberty and privacy. As Adam Moore argues, 'we value national security, not because some specific political union is valuable in itself, but because it is a necessary part of protecting individual rights' (Moore, 2011: 142). The value of the state, and the need for national security, is drawn from the value of those individuals it is charged with protecting: 'whatever rights and privileges states have, they have them only in so far as they thereby serve individuals' fundamental interests' (Fabre, 2008: 964). This includes that security should also involve enabling people's privacy by creating the protections one needs, both physically and symbolically, that prevent outsiders (including the state) from intruding on private spaces or accessing personal information without authorization. At the same time, the interest in autonomy creates the need for protection against manipulation and coercion and promotes the need for individuals to be free-thinking and sufficiently informed in both their personal and political life. And liberty means that people should be able to associate and communicate with those of their choice when it does not cause harm to others.

This reorientation is important as it reframes the relationship between civil liberties and security, and in turn reshapes how the actions of the state and hackers can be understood. For example, state narratives often position it so that liberties need to be traded so people can have physical security. For example, 'after 9/11 countries around the globe unhesitatingly adopted policies to enhance their government's capacity to prevent terrorism ... at the expense of individual civil liberties' (Dragu, 2011; see also Ackerman, 2006). That is, you can either have security or you can have your civil liberties, but you cannot have both (Waldron, 2003). These narratives include a balancing exercise, where a more perfect mid-point between levels of civil liberties and security powers are ever sought and moved, or as a trade-off where one must sacrifice one if we are to have the other (McArthur, 2001; Pozen, 2016). One trade-off often discussed is between privacy and security, where the dichotomy presented is such that you can have either security or privacy and, importantly, where security is seen to be a trump card that overrides other concerns (Thompson, 2001; Dragu, 2011; Bambauer, 2013). This is a particular framing that has always been part of the rhetoric surrounding the debate on security and human rights, but came into stark contrast in the wake of the 9/11 attacks and was propelled into the public narrative following the Snowden leaks (Baker, 2003; Silberstein, 2004). Even if such a framing were correct, Jeremy Waldron warns that it would be problematic as the distribution of the trade-off is unequally felt across society, with minorities suffering the most with no clear return of increased security for themselves. However, more importantly, by reconceptualizing security as the means by which all the vital interests are provided for, the debate shifts towards the overall best conditions for providing for all of these vital interests. This is, therefore, closer to the sentiment outlined in the President's Review Group on Intelligence and Communications Technologies, which noted that while the word 'security' often refers to national or homeland security, it should include those ethical norms vital for 'people to be secure in their persons' (Clarke et al, 2013).

This is important for the approach to political hacking because rather than seeing hackers as a threat to security and society when they act to protect people's liberties, they are in fact providing a more holistic form of security. The security of the individual and the society they are in can be examined in terms of how infringements of vital interests such as liberty and privacy are justified in terms of protecting other vital interests, such as physical integrity; or how violating the privacy of a few specific targets can provide for greater autonomy of many others. This places political hackers not in opposition to the security of the state, but as a tool for providing security to the political community.

Supporting national security leaks

Another key update would be to expand the existing law that allows for whistleblowing in other professions to the currently explicitly discounted realm of national security. Arguably the existing oversight mechanisms are fundamentally ineffective. Current mechanisms rely on those who are expected to keep a watch on the coercive power of the state – for example in terms of national security providers such as the intelligence organizations – and achieve this by having the circle of secrecy extended to cover them. They are brought into the inner circle. However, the result of this is that no one is therefore maintaining a watch over them and their decision-making in this space. They are in fact subjected to many of the same pressures as those within the national security infrastructure, while simultaneously escaping the limiting power of public observation. This allows the opportunity for personal or political biases to flourish. As Kono has argued and demonstrated, electoral systems encourage governments to emphasize policy decisions that please voters while hiding those that go against the majority's will, placing pressure to select the 'correct' message and limit contradicting information (Kono, 2006). This protection undermines the very purpose of external observation by an outside force.

Furthermore, the existing system of separation of power and checks-and-balances has historically been shown to fail in the area of national security. Cultures and practices of compartmentalization, unequal power and access to information between the different branches of government, and a condensing of power in the executive, means that there are no penetrative counter-forces to national security providers. Rahul Sagar offers a detailed and systematic evaluation of this, arguing that 'where the Congress is concerned, its structure and composition ... make it prone to undisciplined disclosures', while also 'Given the President's stronghold over the flow of national security information, there is little reason to believe that lawmakers will be able to *take the lead* in uncovering policies and actions'. For the judiciary he argues that 'judges are not trained, and the courts not equipped, to make politically charged decisions about what state secrets are appropriate' coupled with a 'judicial deference towards the executive's claims about the harm likely to be caused by the disclosures'(Sagar, 2016: 23, 128, 74; see also Fluri and Born, 2003: 22). Kathleen Clark has also written extensively on the executive's failure to act as a suitable counter to national security cultures, arguing that despite President Obama's promise of a 'new era of openness', there were 'disappointments' in his willingness to 'hold accountable those involved in several controversial Bush administration intelligence programs' (Clark, 2010: 315; Clark, 2011). While William Weaver and Robert Pillitto have argued that in the US 'the executive branch over the last several decades have been emboldened to assert secrecy privileged because of judicial timidity and because of Congressional ineffectiveness' (Weaver and Pallitto, 2005: 86). Their conclusion is that 'the privilege is invariably fatal to efforts to gain access to covered documents', that the structures are insufficient to prevent abuse of the privilege as courts are unable to administer costs for misappropriate use, and that because the intelligence services claim that small bits of information are part of a much bigger intelligence secret related to national security, the courts are unable and unwilling to supplant their understanding of national security over that of the intelligence and security infrastructure (Weaver and Pallitto, 2005: 103–4; for more on the institutional arrangement and executive dominance of the classification system, see Morrissey, 1997: 35–7; Brooks, 2004: 2).[3] Indeed, the Edward Snowden revelations demonstrated that there was a systematic and cultural failure to challenge surveillance power as the Foreign Intelligence Surveillance Court was protected from insider judicial peer review and the right to appeal prevented.[4] What this highlights is that these existing political structures lack the physical power to keep the intelligence community in check; are insufficient in manpower, intellectual mandate or drive to do so; or cannot separate their own political interests from their role as overseers. This problem is then heightened even further in instances of private security actors. There is not even the same relationship between the key oversight actors and the private security provider, while arguably they can develop and deploy increasingly powerful cyber-surveillance tools.

---

[3]   On the relationship between the courts and other parts of government, see Dorsen and Shattuck, 1974; Deyling 1992; Fuchs, 2006.

[4]   For the importance of multi-layered court systems, see Dalton, 1985; Nobles and Schiff, 2002; Lennerfors, 2007.

The open-source state

A companion piece to this is the importance of state actors and institutions being as open-source as possible. The police shootings demonstrated a combative culture of hostility between state actors like the police and the communities in which they operate, which are exacerbated by a clear lack of mechanisms for constructively resolving that conflict when issues arise. The main call from the protestors, activists and hackers was one of transparency, action and engagement. They wanted to see justice being performed. Making the process, evidence and decisions as open and accessible as possible can play an important role. It provides greater opportunity for engagement by other people, promotes discussion and critique of the evidence provided, and means that alternative views can be shared and gain wider support for the decision made.

Conclusion

The relationship between the state and non-state actors wielding political violence is always going to be fraught. Traditional conceptions that locate legitimate political violence only in the hands of the state ignore the threat that the state itself can represent. Top-down and narrow conceptualizations of security place the state as both the main target and provider of security and so prioritize conceptions of physical protection and defence for the state's infrastructures as the sole target for protective efforts, much to the cost of other vital interests. This in turn feeds into a hyper-securitized fear of hackers who are seen as the antithesis of what security is and represent an unknown threat, especially with officials and media portraying near-apocalyptic abilities. However, in reality political hackers have neither the ability nor the will to bring about that level of destruction, and this book is not arguing that such actions can be ethically justified. The approach, both legal and political, to political hackers is therefore significantly out of sync. In practice political hackers have demonstrated a consistent approach to acting for people's core vital interests, and even though they have caused instances of unjustified harm, it pales in comparison to the punishments delivered.

Conclusion

The nature of political hacking represents a clear challenge to the legitimate use of political violence. It acts outside the traditional state infrastructures and mechanisms, and often against the state itself, which for many means that regardless of what good it brings it should be ethically discounted as an illegitimate actor threatening the social stability. Concerns over the ability of hackers to cause significant damage or harm to people's lives and the critical infrastructure of the political community do have some merit. They are a highly closeted, elite and unknown quantity; their branding is menacing and for those on the outside there does not seem to be any means of controlling what they do. Indeed, the state has a long-held dominance as the only legitimate actor to use violence for good reason, including protecting people from harm, arbitrating disagreements and facilitating that the correct quantum of impact is being delivered to the correct people. However, this is becoming increasingly challenged, not least because the state and its representatives have shown themselves to be a direct threat to people's vital interests. As such there can be an ethical space for political hacking when it acts to protect people from harm.

In order to make this determination, however, there is a need for an explicit and systematic ethical framework that can recognize the ethical value of political hacking. One which helps guide the hacker community with clearer fundamental ethical principles, as well as how these principles can then be manifested in various mechanisms for guiding ethical behaviour, highlighting to the rest of the political community when to leave the hackers alone, and how this might work through real-world illustrative examples.

It has therefore been argued that the state should not be the only actor to use political violence and that its own use is not inherently legitimate without qualification. Its value is drawn from the role it plays in representing and protecting the political community. When it fails in this role, either generally or in specific instances, then others can and should act – including hackers. Therefore, at its core, there is a value in protecting people from harm regardless of who it is that delivers that protection. This right to the defence of others means that hackers can use political violence against those who represent a sufficient level of threat.

In Chapter 1, part of this work has included a more detailed understanding of what political hacking means. It argued that it is not necessary for hackers to have a fixed political ideology, but rather that it is possible to understand and judge their political actions as they move from operation to operation. A key contribution was a recognition that the political violence used by hackers varies depending on what they do and against whom, and that, as such, a spectrum of violence could be conceptualized to better understand political hacking operations. This spectrum approach to detailing the way political hacking worked allowed Chapter 2 to create a similar graded approach to the justifying ethical framework. That is, Chapter 2 first argued that hackers could be justified when they protected people from harm, but that their actions needed to be proportional, only used when other actions were redundant, and only against those who were legitimate targets. From here it was also argued that because the level of political violence caused by the hacking varied, so should the justification. When the level of threat being defended against was low, so should be the damage caused by the hack, but when the threat was high, so could be the negative impact of the hack.

This created an ethical framework that allowed Chapters 3, 4 and 5 to explore some of the most prominent political hacking cases. Chapter 3 focused on the importance of political autonomy through the right to association, expression and information rights, arguing that these were fundamental interests for people and so needed protecting when other actors threatened them. Chapter 4 argued that transparency is important, especially in terms of the state's national security apparatus and role, and that as such there was a general right to be informed, especially when there were instances of wrongdoing. This justified the use of whistleblowing by an organization's internal actors, as well as penetrating an organization (both state and private) when there was evidence that they represented a threat of some form. However, when applied to civilians, often they would not represent a sufficient threat to overcome their right to privacy. Chapter 5 then expanded this discussion to look at non-cyber, non-informational cases where people's vital interests were threatened. It was argued that this should include when the state represents a threat through unjustified laws, policies, procedures or cultures, or when the state had failed in its role of providing and enacting good social laws and practices.

Finally, Chapter 6 allowed the opportunity to circle back to the ethical framework and examine its broader contributions following the application to illustrative examples. This chapter discussed the dangers of abusing the ethical framework when the ethical criteria are not properly engaged with and used as a superficial cover through a 'tick-box' exercise to justify unethical (selfish) behaviour. It argued that the concept of right intention acted as a means of making sure that the ethical criteria were used correctly. That the right intention, justification and methods/targets chosen must all be reflective of each other, whereby the right intention must flow from the justification (defence) and then be reflected in what is done and to whom. Chapter 6 also provided an explanation of the current heightened fear of hacking by society and political elites, and how this was dramatically distorting the subsequent legal punishments being issued, despite there being little actual cause for this framing. As such, it argued that the legal, political and social approach to hacking needed to be updated by creating a greater understanding of the variety of ways in which political hacking can be used and the impacts it can have, and that consequently a more nuanced approach to its use was needed. And finally, it argued that the argument for self-defence needed to be more explicitly embedded in our understanding of hacking so that, even when harm or damaged is done, the hackers can be seen as justified in their actions.

References

Abbott, T. G., Lai, K. J., Lieberman, M. R. and Price, E. C. (2007) 'Browser based attacks on TOR', *Privacy Enhancing Technologies*, 4776 (June): 184–99.

Ackerman, B. (2006) *Before the Next Attack: Preserving Civil Liberties in the Age of Terrorism*, New Haven, CT: Yale University Press.

Adams, J. (2013) 'Decriminalizing hacktivism: finding space for free speech protests on the internet', *SSRN*, 15 December. Available from: https://ssrn.com/abstract=2392945

Agrawal, T., Henry, D. and Finkle, J. (2014) 'JPMorgan hack exposed data of 83 million, among biggest breaches in history', *Reuters*, 3 October. Available from: https://www.reuters.com/article/us-jpmorgan-cybersecurity-idUSKCN0HR23T20141003

Alexander, L. (1976) 'Self-defence and the killing of non-combatants: a reply to Fullinwider', *Philosophy and Public Affairs*, 5(4): 408–15.

Alexopoulou, S. and Pavli, A. (2019) '"Beneath this mask there is more than flesh, beneath this mask there is an idea": anonymous as the (super)heroes of the internet?', *International Journal for the Semiotics of Law*, 34: 237–64.

Altman, I. (1976) 'Privacy: a conceptual analysis', *Environment and Behaviour*, 8(1): 7.

Alvarez, A. and Bachman, R. (2007) *Violence: The Enduring Problem*, London: Sage.

Ambinder, M. and Grady, D. (2013) *Deep State: Inside the Government Secrecy Industry*, Hoboken, NJ: John Wiley & Sons Inc.

Anderson, L. (2011) 'Demystifying the Arab Spring: parsing the differences between Tunisia, Egypt, and Libya', *Foreign Affairs*, 90(3): 2–7.

Anderson, N. (2011) 'How one man tracked down Anonymous – and paid a heavy price', *Ars Technica*, 9 February. Available from: https://arstechnica.com/tech-policy/2011/02/how-one-security-firm-tracked-anonymousand-paid-a-heavy-price/

Anonymous (2011) 'AnonNews.org: everything Anonymous'. Available from: http://anonnews.org/press/item/199/

Aquinas, T. (2002) 'From *Summa Theologiae*', in C. Brown, T. Nardin and N. Rengger (eds), *International Relations in Political Thought*, Cambridge: Cambridge University Press, pp 213–20.

Arendt, H. (1979) *The Origins of Totalitarianism*, London: Harcourt, Brace & World.

Ars (2011) 'Anonymous speaks: the inside story of the HBGary Hack', ARSTechnica, 16 February. Available from: https://arstechnica.com/tech-policy/2011/02/anonymous-speaks-the-inside-story-of-the-hbgary-hack/

Arthur, C. (2013) 'LulzSec: what they did, who they were and how they were caught', *The Guardian*, 16 May. Available from: https://www.theguardian.com/technology/2013/may/16/lulzsec-hacking-fbi-jail

Atkin, Lord (1932) *Donoghue v Stevenson*, UKHL 100, 26 May.

Auty, C. (2004) 'Political hacktivism: tool of the underdog or scourge of cyberspace?', *New Information Perspectives*, 56(4): 212–21.

Avant, D. D. (2005) *The Market for Force: The Consequences of Privatizing Security*, Cambridge: Cambridge University Press.

Baber, H. E. (1987) 'How bad is rape', *Hypatia*, 2(2): 125–38.

Baker, C. E. (1978) 'Scope of the First Amendment freedom of speech', *UCLA Law Review*, 25: 964–90.

Baker, N. (2003) 'National security versus civil liberties', *Presidential Studies Quarterly*, 33(3): 547–67.

Baldino, D. (2010) *Democratic Oversight of Intelligence Services*, Sydney: The Federation Press.

Bambauer, D. E. (2013) 'Privacy versus security', *The Journal of Criminal Law and Criminology*, 103(3): 667–83.

Bamford, J. (2013) 'NSA snooping was only the beginning. Meet the spy chief leading us into cyberwar', *Wired*, 12 June. Available from: https://www.wired.com/2013/06/general-keith-alexander-cyberwar/

Bandura, A. (1986) *Social Foundations of Thought and Action: A Social Cognitive Theory*, Englewood Cliffs, NJ: Prentice Hall.

Bandura, A. (1999) 'Moral disengagement in the perpetration of inhumanities', *Personality and Social Psychology Review*, 3(3): 193–209.

Bangkok Post (2015) 'International hackers strike', *Bangkok Post*, 22 October. Available from: http://www.bangkokpost.com/tech/local-news/739884/anonymous-steps-up-single-gateway-protest

Bansal, A. and Arora, M. (2012) 'Ethical hacking and social security', *Journal of Radix International Educational and Research Consortium*, 1(11): 1–16.

Barber, R. (2001) 'Hackers profiled: who are they and what are their motivations?', *Computer Fraud and Security*, 2(1): 14–17.

Bauman, Z., Bigo, D., Esteves, P., Guild, E., Jabri, V., Lyon, D. et al (2014) 'After Snowden: rethinking the impact of surveillance', *International Political Sociology*, 8: 121–44.

BBC News (2007) 'Estonia hit by 'Moscow cyber war', 17 May. Available from: http://news.bbc.co.uk/1/hi/world/europe/6665145.stm

BBC News (2011) 'China hit-and-run driver sentenced to six years in jail', 30 January. Available from: https://www.bbc.co.uk/news/world-asia-pacific-12317756

BBC News (2012) 'Chinese websites defaced in anonymous attack', 5 April. Available from: http://www.bbc.co.uk/news/technology-17623939

BBC News (2019) 'Extinction Rebellion protests: what happened?', 25 April. Available from: https://www.bbc.co.uk/news/uk-england-48051776

Beaney, W. (1966) 'The right to privacy and American law', *Law and Contemporary Problems*, 31: 253–71.

Bellaby, R. W. (2014) *The Ethics of Intelligence: A New Framework*, Abingdon: Routledge.

Bellaby, R. W. (2016) 'Justifying cyber-intelligence?', *Journal of Military Ethics*, 15(4): 299–319.

Bellaby, R. W. (2018) 'Extraordinary rendition: expanding the circle of blame in international politics', *The International Journal of Human Rights*, 22(2): 574–602.

Bellaby, R. W. (2021) 'An ethical framework for hacking operations', *Ethical and Theory Moral Practice*, 24: 231–55.

Bellamy, A. J. (2006) *Just Wars: From Cicero to Iraq*, Cambridge and Malden, MA: Polity Press.

Benn, S. (1971) 'Privacy, freedom and respect for persons', in J. R. Pennock and J. W. Chapman (eds), *Nomos XIII: Privacy*, New York: Atherton Press, pp 1–26.

Berlin, I. (1969) *Four Essays on Liberty*, Oxford: Oxford University Press.

Berman, M. N. (2011) 'Two kinds of retributivism', in R.A. Duff and S. Green (eds), *Philosophical Foundations of Criminal Law*, New York: Oxford University Press, pp 433–57.

Berman, M. N. (2013) 'Rehabilitating retributivism', *Law and Philosophy*, 32: 83–108.

Beyer, J. L. (2014) *Expect Us: Online Communities and Political Marginalisation*, Oxford: Oxford University Press.

Beytagh, F. (1975) 'Privacy and the free press: a contemporary conflict in values', *New York Law Forum*, 20(3): 453–514.

Blasi, V. (1977) 'The checking value in first amendment theory', *American Bar Foundation Research Journal*, 3: 521–649.

Blomfield, A. (2007) 'Estonia calls for NATO cyber-terrorism strategy', *The Telegraph*, 18 May. Available from: https://www.telegraph.co.uk/news/worldnews/1551963/Estonia-calls-for-Nato-cyber-terrorism-strategy.html

Bloustein, E. J. (1978) 'Group privacy: the right to huddle', in E. Bloustein (ed.), *Individual and Group Privacy*, New Brunswick, NJ: Transaction Books, pp 123–87.

Bok, S. (1985) 'Distrust, secrecy and the arms race', *Ethics*, 95(3): 712–27.

Bollinger, L. (1986) *The Tolerant Society: Freedom of Speech and Extremist Speech in America*, Oxford: Oxford University Press.

Bolsin, S., Pal, R., Wilmhurst, P. and Pena, M. (2011) 'Whistleblowing and patient safety: the patient's or the profession's interests at stake?', *Journal of the Royal Society of Medicine*, 104: 278–82.

Borsook, P. (2000) *Cyberselfish: A Critical Romp through the Terribly Libertarian Culture of High Tech*, New York: PublicAffairs.

Bouville, M. (2008) 'Whistleblowing and morality', *Journal of Business Ethics*, 81: 579–85.

Bowie, N. (1982) *Business Ethics*, Englewood Cliffs, NJ: Prentice-Hall.

Boyle, J. (1997) *Shamans, Software and Spleens: Law and the Construction of the Information Society*, Cambridge, MA, and London: Harvard University Press.

Braham, M. and van Hees, M. (2012) 'An anatomy of moral responsibility', *Mind*, 121(483): 601–34.

Brandeis, L. and Warren, S. (1980) 'The right to privacy', *The Harvard Law Review*, 4(5): 193–220.

Breckenridge, A. C. (1970) *The Right to Privacy*, Lincoln: University of Nebraska Press.

Brenkert, G. (2010) 'Whistle-blowing, moral integrity, and organizational ethics', in G. Brenkert and T. L. Beauchamp (eds), *The Oxford Handbook of Business Ethics*, New York: Oxford University Press, pp 563–601.

Breslin, V. and Dooley, J. (2002) 'Whistle blowing v. confidentiality: can circumstances mandate attorneys to expose their clients?', *Georgetown Journal of Legal Ethics*, 15(4): 719–40.

Brison, S. J. (1998a) 'The autonomy defence of free speech', *Ethics*, 108(2): 312–39.

Brison, S. J. (1998b) 'Speech, harm, and the mind-body problem in First Amendment jurisprudence', *Legal Theory*, 4(1): 39–61.

Brocklebank, C. (2012) 'Anonymous hack into Ugandan government websites in protest at their anti-LGBT policies', *Pink News*, 15 August. Available from: https://www.pinknews.co.uk/2012/08/15/anonymous-hack-into-ugandan-government-websites-in-protest-at-their-anti-lgbt-policies/

Brooking, E. T. (2015) 'Anonymous vs. the Islamic State', *Foreign Policy*. Available from: http://foreignpolicy.com/2015/11/13/anonymous-hackers-islamic-state-isis-chan-online-war/

Brooks, N. (2004) *The Protection of Classified Information: The Legal Framework*, Washington, DC: Congressional Research Service.

Brownlee, K. (2012) *Conscience and Conviction: The Case for Civil Disobedience*, Oxford: Oxford University Press.

Brownlee, K. (2016) 'The civil disobedience of Edward Snowden: a reply to William Scheuerman', *Philosophy and Social Criticism*, 42(10): 965–70.

Bueza, M. (2016) 'Is Comelec liable for website data leak?', *Rappler*, 11 April. Available from: https://www.rappler.com/newsbreak/in-depth/127465-comelec-hackers-liability-website-hacking-data-leak

Bufacchi, V. (2005) 'Two concepts of violence', *Political Studies Review*, 3(2): 193–204.

Butler, J. (2004) *Precarious Lives: The Powers of Mourning and Violence*, London: Verso.

Cardwell, T. (2011) 'Ethical hackers: putting on the white', *Network Security*, July: 1–13.

Carr, I. and Lewis, D. (2010) 'Combating corruption through employment law and whistleblower protection', *Industrial Law Journal*, 39(1): 1–30.

Carr, L. (1998) 'Tomboy resistance and conformity: agency in social psychological gender theory', *Gender & Society*, 12: 528–53.

Casserly, M. (2015) 'Who is Anonymous? A short history of hacktivism', *Tech Advisor*, 18 November. Available from: https://www.techadvisor. com/feature/internet/what-is-hacktivism-short-history-anonymous-lulz sec-arab-spring-3414409/#ixzz2lt9LEheM

Celikates, R. (2015) 'Digital publics, digital contestation: a new structural transformation', in R. Celikates, R. Kreide and T. Wesche (eds), *Transformations of Democracy: Crisis, Protest and Legitimation*, London: Rowman and Littlefield, pp 159–76.

Celikates, R. (2016) 'Rethinking civil disobedience as a practice of contestation', *Constellations*, 23(1): 37–45.

Cha, A. and Nakashima, E. (2010) 'Google China cyberattack part of spy campaign', *NBC News*, 14 January. Available from: https://www.nbcnews. com/id/wbna34855470

Chambers, S. (2004) 'Behind closed doors: publicity, secrecy, and the quality of deliberation', *The Journal of Political Philosophy*, 12(4): 389–410.

Cheung, A. S. Y. (2009) 'China internet going wild: cyber-hunting versus privacy protection', *Computer Law and Security Review*, 25: 275–79.

China.org.cn (2010) 'Drunken driver arrested for fatal incident', 26 October. Available from: http://www.china.org.cn/china/2010-10/26/content_2 1200529.htm

Chirinos, C. (2022) 'Anonymous takes revenge on Putin's brutal Ukraine invasion by leaking personal data of 120,000 russian soldiers', *Fortune*, 4 April. Available from: https://fortune.com/2022/04/04/anonymous-leaks-russian-soldier-data-ukraine-invasion/

Christopher, R. (1998) 'Self-defense and defense of others', *Philosophy and Public Affairs*, 27(2): 123–41.

Citron, D. K. (2014) *Hate Crimes in Cyberspace*, Cambridge, MA: Harvard University Press.

Clark, K. (2010) '"A new era of openness?" Disclosing intelligence to Congress under Obama', *Constitutional Commentary*, 26: 313–37.

Clark, K. (2011) 'Congress's right to counsel intelligence oversight', *University of Illinois Law Review*, 2011(3): 915–60.

Clarke, R., Morell, M. J., Stone, G. R., Sunstein, C. R. and Swire, P. (2013) *President's Review Group on Intelligence and Communications Technologies, Liberty and Security in a Changing World*. Available from: https://obamawhiteho use.archives.gov/sites/default/files/docs/2013-12-12_rg_final_report.pdf

CNN Wire Staff (2011) 'Hackers target San Francisco's Rapid Transit System', *CNN*, 16 August. Available from: http://edition.cnn.com/2011/ US/08/14/california.transit.hack/index.html

Coates, A. J. (1997) *The Ethics of War*, Manchester: Manchester University Press.

Cohen, C. (1970) 'Defending civil disobedience', *The Monist*, 54(4): 469–87.

Cohen, J. (1993) 'Freedom of expression', *Philosophy and Public Affairs*, 22(3): 207–63.

Coleman, G. (2011) 'Hacker politics and publics', *Public Culture*, 23(3): 511–16.

Coleman, G. (2014) *Hacker, Hoaxer, Whistleblower, Spy: The Many Faces of Anonymous*, London: Verso.

Coleman, G. (2022) 'The public interest hack', *Lima*, 8. Available from: https://limn.it/articles/the-public-interest-hack/

Conway, M. (2003) 'Hackers or terrorists? Why it doesn't compute', *Computer Fraud and Security*, 12: 10–13.

Copp, D. (1991) 'Responsibility for collective inaction', *Journal of Social Philosophy*, 22(2): 71–80.

Critical Art Ensemble (1996) *Electronic Civil Disobedience and Other Unpopular Ideas*, New York: Autonomedia.

Crosston, M. (2017) 'The fight for cyber Thoreau: distinguishing virtual disobedience from digital destruction', in M. Korstanje (ed.), *Threat Mitigation and Detection of Cyber Warfare and Terrorism Activities*, Hershey, PA: IGI Global, pp 198–219.

Dalton, H. L. (1985) 'Taking the right to appeal (more or less) seriously', *Yale Law Journal*, 95(1): 62–107.

Darby, J. (2016) 'Political violence: an overview', in M. Breen-Smyth (ed.), *The Ashgate Research Companion to Political Violence*, London: Routledge, pp 17–32.

Davis, M. (1996) 'Some paradoxes of whistleblowing', *Business & Professional Ethics Journal*, 15(1): 3–19.

DeGeorge, R. (1981) 'Ethical responsibilities of engineers in large organizations: the Pinto case', *Business & Professional Ethics Journal*, 1(1): 1–14.

DeGeorge, R. (1990) *Business Ethics*, Basingstoke: Palgrave MacMillan.

Della Porta, D. (1995) *Social Movements, Political Violence, and the State: A Comparative Analysis of Italy and Germany*, New York: Cambridge University Press.

Delmas, C. (2018a) 'Is hacktivism the new civil disobedience?', *Raisons Politiques*, 69(1): 63–81.

Delmas, C. (2018b) *A Duty to Resist: When Disobedience Should be Uncivil*, Oxford: Oxford University Press.

Dempsey, J. X. and Flint, L. M. (2004) 'Commercial data and national security', *The George Washington Law Review*, 72: 1459–502.

Denning, D. (1999) 'Activism, hacktivism and cyber-terrorism: the internet as a tool for influencing foreign policy', *Global Problem Solving Information Technology and Tools*, 10 December. Available from: https://nautilus.org/global-problem-solving/activism-hacktivism-and-cyberterrorism-the-internet-as-a-tool-for-influencing-foreign-policy-2/

Denning, D. (2010) 'Terror's web: how the internet is transforming terrorism', in Y. Jewkes and M. Yar (eds), *Handbook of Internet Crime*, Cullompton: Willan Publishing, pp 194–213.

Dewey, J. (1980) 'Force, violence and law' and 'Force and coercion', in J. A. Boydston (ed.), John Dewey, *The Middle Works*, 1899–1924, Volume 10: 1916–1917, Carbondale, IL: Southern Illinois University Press.

Deyling, R. (1992) 'Judicial deference and de novo review in litigation over national security information under the Freedom of Information Act', *Villanova Law Review*, 37(1): 67–112.

Dittrich, D. and Himma, K. (2006) 'Hackers, crackers and common criminals', in H. Bidgoli (ed.), *Handbook of Information Security: Information Warfare; Social Issues, Legal and International Issues; and Security Foundations, Vol.2*, Hoboken, NJ: Wiley, pp 154–71.

Dorsen, N. and Shattuck, J. H. F. (1974) 'Executive privilege, the Congress and the courts', *Ohio State Law Journal*, 35(1): 1–40.

Douglas, D. M. (2016) 'Doxxing: a conceptual analysis', *Ethics and Information Technology*, 19: 199.

Dragu, T. (2011) 'Is there a trade-off between security and liberty? Executive bias, privacy protections, and terrorism prevention', *American Political Science Review*, 105(1): 64–78.

Duff, A. (2011) 'Retrieving retributivism', in M. White (ed.), *Retributivism: Essays on Theory and Policy*, Oxford: Oxford University Press.

Dumsday, T. (2009) 'On cheering Charles Bronson: the ethics of vigilantism', *The Southern Journal of Philosophy*, 47(1): 49–67.

Dunaway, W. (1996) 'Incorporation as an interactive process: Cherokee resistance to expansion of the capitalist world-system, 1560–1763', *Sociological Inquiry*, 66: 455–70.

Dunfee, T. W. and Maurer, V. G. (1992) 'Corporate attorney whistle-blowing: devising a proper standard', *Business & Professional Ethics Journal*, 11(3): 3–39.

Dworkin, R. (1985) *A Matter of Principle*, Cambridge, MA: Harvard University Press.

Eckert, A. E. (2020) 'The changing nature of legitimate authority in the just war tradition', *Journal of Military Ethics*, 19(2): 84–98.

The Economist (2011) 'Leaks must not poison diplomacy', 27 January. Available from: http://www.economist.com/nodc/18010593

Edstein, R. A. (1992) 'Property speech and the politics of distrust', *The Bill of Rights in the Welfare State: A Bicentennial Symposium*, 59(1): 41–89.

Eleftheriou-Smith, L. (2015) 'Anonymous calls for activists to help expose international paedophile networks with "Operation DeathEaters"', *The Independent*, 23 January. Available from: https://www.independent.co.uk/news/uk/home-news/anonymous-calls-activists-help-expose-international-paedophile-networks-operation-deatheaters-9998350.html

Elliott, C. (2013) 'WikiLeaks and the public interest dilemma: a view from inside the media', in B. Benedetta, A. Hintz and P. McCurdy (eds), *Beyond Wikileaks: Implications for the Future of Communications, Journalism and Society*, Basingstoke: Palgrave Macmillan, pp 78–84.

Emerson, T. I. (1964) 'Freedom of association and freedom of expression', *The Yale Law Journal*, 74(1): 1–64.

Emerson, T. I. (1970) *The System of Freedom of Expression*, New York: Vintage.

Emerson, T. I. (1976) 'Legal foundations of the right to know', *Washington University Law Quarterly*, 1: 1–24.

Emspak, J. (2011) 'Update: Egyptian gov't web sites under attack', *International Business Times*, 26 January. Available from: http://www.ibtimes.com/articles/105329/20110126/update-egyptian-gov-t-web-sites-under-attack.htm

Fabre, C. (2008) 'Cosmopolitanism, just war tradition and legitimate authority', *International Affairs*, 84(5): 963–76.

Fabre, C. (2012) *Cosmopolitan War*, Oxford: Oxford University Press

Fabre, C. (2018) *Economic Statecraft: Human Rights, Sanctions, and Conditionality*, Cambridge, MA: Harvard University Press.

Fairfield, P. (2005) *Public/Private*, London: Rowman & Littlefield Publishers.

Farsole, A., Kashikar, A. G. and Zunzunwala, A. (2010) 'Ethical hacking', *International Journal of Computer Applications*, 1(10): 14–20.

Farwell, J. and Rohozinski, R. (2011) 'Stuxnet and the future of cyber war', *Survival: Global Politics and Strategy*, 53(1): 24–5.

Fein, H. (2007) *Human Rights and Wrongs: Slavery, Terror and Genocide*, Boulder, CO: Paradigm Publishers.

Feinberg, J. (1973) 'The idea of a free man', in J. F. Doyle (ed), *Educational Judgments: Papers in the Philosophy of Education*, London: Routledge, pp 143–65.

Feinberg, J. (1984) *Moral Limits of the Criminal Law, Vol.1: Harm to Others*, Oxford: Oxford University Press.

Finn, P. (2009) 'GOP senators drop out of panel inquiry into CIA program', *The Washington Post*, 26 September. Available from: http://www.washing tonpost.com/wp-dyn/content/article/2009/09/25/AR2009092503 745.html

Fitri, N. (2011) 'Democracy discourses through the internet communication: understanding the hacktivism for the global changing', *Online Journal of Communication and Media Technologies*, 1(2): 1–20.

Fixdall, M. and Smith, D. (1998) 'Humanitarian intervention and just war', *Mershon International Studies Review*, 42(2): 283–312.

Fleddermann, C. (1999) *Engineering Ethics*, Englewood Cliffs, NJ: Prentice Hall.

FLSnag (2011) 'I am one Anonymous', *YouTube*, 23 July. Available from: http://www.youtube.com/watch?v=aEcvaoDIKtU

Fluri, P. and Born, H. (2003) *Parliamentary Oversight of the Security Sector: Principles Mechanisms and Practices*, Geneva: DCAF.

Ford, Z. (2012) 'Anonymous hacks Ugandan government in retaliation for anti-LGBT policies', *Think Progress*, 14 August. Available from: https:// thinkprogress.org/anonymous-hacks-ugandan-government-in-retaliation-for-anti-lgbt-policies-8d31d15aa874#.cbrcmbr9c

Foucault, M. (1979) *Discipline and Punish: The Birth of the Prison*, Harmondsworth: Penguin.

Frankfurt, H. (1971) 'Freedom of the will and the concept of the person', *Journal of Philosophy*, 68(1): 5–20.

Fried, C. (1968) 'Privacy: a moral analysis', *Yale Law Review*, 77(1): 475–93.

Fried, C. (1992) 'The new First Amendment jurisprudence: a threat to liberty', in G. R. Stone, R. A. Epstein and C. R. Sunstein (eds), *The Bill of Rights in the Modern State*, Chicago, IL: University of Chicago Press, pp 225–53.

Fuchs, C. (2013) 'The Anonymous movement in the context of liberalism and socialism', *Interface*, 5(2): 345–76.

Fuchs, M. (2006) 'Judging secrets: the role courts should play in preventing unnecessary secrecy', *Administrative Law Review*, 58(1): 131–76.

Gandy, O. (2003) 'Data mining and surveillance in the post 9/11 environment', in K. Bell and F. Webster (eds), *The Intensification of Surveillance: Crime, Terrorism and Warfare in the Information Age*, London and Sterling, VA: Pluto Press, pp 363–84.

Gerwehr, S. and Daly, S. (2006) 'Al-Qaida: terrorist selection and recruitment', in D. Kamien (ed.), *The McGraw-Hill Homeland Security Handbook*, New York: McGraw-Hill, pp 73–89.

Gewirth, A. (1978) *Reason and Morality*, Chicago, IL: University of Chicago Press.

Glave, J. (1998) 'Crackers: we stole nuke data', *Wired*, 3 June. Available from: https://www.wired.com/1998/06/crackers-we-stole-nuke-data/

Goldschlag, D., Reed, M. and Syverson, P. (1999) 'Onion routing for anonymous and private internet connections', *Communications of the ACM*, 42(2): 39–41.

Golumbia, D. (2013) 'Cyberlibertarianism: the extremist foundations of "digital freedom"', *Uncomputing*. Available from: http://www.academia.edu/4429212/Cyberlibertarianism_The_Extremist_Foundations_of_Digital_Freedom

Goode, L. (2015) 'Anonymous and the political ethos of hacktivism', *Popular Communication: The International Journal of Media and Culture*, 13(1): 74–86.

Gorman, S. (2012) 'Alert on hacker power play: US official signals growing concern over anonymous group's capabilities', *The Wall Street Journal*, 21 February. Available from: https://www.wsj.com/articles/SB10001424052970204059804577229390105521090

Gray, P. W. (2013) 'Leaderless resistance, networked organisation, and ideological hegemony', *Terrorism and Political Violence*, 25(5): 655–71.

Greenberg, A. (2012a) *This Machine Kills Secrets: Julian Assange, the Cypherpunks, and Their Fight to Empower Whistleblowers*, New York: Penguin Group.

Greenberg, A. (2012b) 'Anonymous hackers swat at Syrian government websites in reprisal for internet blackout', *Forbes*, 30 November. Available from: http://www.forbes.com/sites/andygreenberg/2012/11/30/anonymous-hackers-swat-at-syrian-government-websites-in-reprisal-for-internet-blackout/#105975b4418f

Greenwald, G. (2011) 'The leaked campaign to attack Wikileaks and its supporters', *Salon.com*, 11 February. Available from: https://www.salon.com/2011/02/11/campaigns_4/

Greenwalt, K. (1989) 'Free speech justifications', *Columbia Law Review*, 89(1): 119–55.

Gregg, N. (1993) '"Trying to put first things first": negotiating subjectivities in a workplace organizing campaign', in S. Fisher and K. Davis (eds), *Negotiating at the Margins: The Gendered Discourses of Power and Resistance*, New Brunswick, NJ: Rutgers University Press, pp 172–204.

Griffin, A. (2016) 'WhatsApp end-to-end encryption update might have made chat app illegal in India', *Independent*, 8 April. Available from: http://www.independent.co.uk/life-style/gadgets-and-tech/news/whatsapp-end-to-end-encryption-update-might-have-made-chat-app-illegal-in-india-a6974921.html

Griswold, E. N. (1989) 'Secrets not worth keeping', *The Washington Post*, 15 February. Available from: https://www.washingtonpost.com/archive/opinions/1989/02/15/secrets-not-worth-keeping/a115a154-4c6f-41fd-816a-112dd9908115/

Grofman, B., Owen, G. and Feld, S. (1983) 'Thirteen theorems in search of the truth', *Theory and Decision*, 15: 261–78.

Gross, H. (1971) 'Privacy and autonomy', in J. R. Pennock and J. W. Chapman (eds), *Privacy: Nomos XIII*, New York: Atherton Press, pp 169–81.

Habermas, J. (1996) *Between Facts and Norms: Contributions to a Discourse Theory of Law and Democracy*, Cambridge: Polity Press.

Halliday, J. (2011) 'Anonymous hackers breach San Francisco BART transport website', *The Guardian*, 15 August. Available from: https://www.theguardian.com/technology/2011/aug/15/anonymous-hackers-breach-bart-website

Halliday, J. and Arthur, C. (2010) 'Wikileaks: who are the hackers behind Operation Payback?', *The Guardian*, 8 December. Available from: https://www.theguardian.com/media/2010/dec/08/anonymous-4chan-wikileaks-mastercard-paypal

Hampson, N. (2012) 'Hacktivism: a new breed of protest in a networked world', *Boston College International and Comparative Law Review*, 35(2): 511–42.

Harding, L. and Leigh, D. (2011) 'Wikileaks: how US political invective turned on "anti-American" Julian Assange', *The Guardian*, 3 February. Available from: https://www.theguardian.com/world/2011/feb/03/wikileaks-julian-assange-us-reaction

Harmon, A. (1999) '"Hacktivists" of all persuasions take their struggle to the web', *The New York Times*, 31 October. Available from: http://www.nytimes.com/1998/10/31/world/hacktivists-of-all-persuasions-take-their-struggle-to-the-web.html

Harris, C., Pritchard, M. S. and Rabins, M. J. (2005) *Engineering Ethics: Concepts and Cases*, Belmont, CA: Wadsworth.

Harris, D. (1999) 'Driving while black and other traffic offences: the Supreme Court and pretextual traffic stops', *The Journal of Criminal Law and Criminology*, 87: 544–82.

Harris, D. (2002) 'Racial profiling revisited: "just common sense" in the fight against terror?', *Criminal Justice*, 17: 36–59.

Hausman, D. and McPhereson, M. (1996) *Economic Analysis and Moral Philosophy*, Cambridge: Cambridge University Press.

Heinze, E. and Steel, B. J. (eds) (2009) *Ethics, Authority, and War: Non-State Actors and the Just War Tradition*, New York: Palgrave Macmillan.

Hendler, J. (2013) 'It's time to reform the Computer Fraud and Abuse Act', *Scientific American*, 16 August. Available from: https://www.scientificamerican.com/article/its-times-reform-computer-fraud-abuse-act/

Herman, B. (1996) *The Practice of Moral Judgement*, Cambridge, MA: Harvard University Press.

Hern, A. (2015) 'Anonymous "at war" with Isis, hacktivist group confirms', *The Guardian*, 17 December. Available from: https://www.theguardian.com/technology/2015/nov/17/anonymous-war-isis-hacktivist-group-confirms

Hern, A. (2016) 'Islamic State Twitter account gets a rainbow makeover from Anonymous', *The Guardian*, 17 June. Available from: https://www.theguardian.com/technology/2016/jun/17/islamic-state-twitter-accounts-rainbow-makeover-anonymous-hackers

Hersh, M. (2002) 'Whistle-blowers: heroes or traitors? Individual and collective responsibility for ethical behaviour', *Annual Reviews in Control*, 26: 243–62.

Higgins, P. (2013) 'Critical fixes for the Computer Fraud and Abuse Act', *Electronic Frontier Foundation*, 29 January. Available from: https://www.eff.org/deeplinks/2013/01/these-are-critical-fixes-computer-fraud-and-abuse-act

Hill, E. (2011a) 'Hackers hit Tunisian websites', *Al Jazeera*, 3 January. Available from: https://www.aljazeera.com/news/2011/1/3/hackers-hit-tunisian-websites

Hill, E. (2011b) 'How "rebel" phone network evaded shutdown', *Al Jazeera*, 23 April. Available from: http://www.aljazeera.com/indepth/features/2011/04/20114233530919767.html

Himma, K. (2005) 'Hacking as politically motivated digital civil disobedience: is hacktivism morally justified?', *SSRN*, 5 September. Available from: https://ssrn.com/abstract=799545

Himma, K. (2008) 'Ethical issues involving computer security: hacking, hacktivism, and counterhacking', in K. Himma and H. Tavani (eds), *The Handbook of Information and Computer Ethics*, Hoboken, NJ: Wiley.

Hine, K. D. (1998) 'Vigilantism revisited: an economic analysis of the law of extra-judicial self-help or why can't Dick shoot Henry for stealing Jane's truck', *American University Law Review*, 47: 1221–55.

von Hirsch, A. (2000) 'The ethics of public television surveillance', in A Hirsch, D. Garland and A. Wakefield (eds), *Ethical and Social Perspectives on Situational Crime Prevention*, Oxford: Hart Publishing, pp 59–76.

Hobbes, T. (1985) [1651] *Leviathan*, London: Penguin Classics.

Hoffman, W. M. (1984) 'The Ford Pinto', in W. Hoffman, and J. Moore (eds), *Business Ethics: Readings and Cases in Corporate Morality*, New York: Wiley, pp 249–60.

Hohfeld, W. N. (1913) 'Some fundamental legal conceptions as applied in judicial reasoning', *Yale Law Journal*, 23: 16–59.

Hollander, J. A. and Einwohner, R. L. (2004) 'Conceptualising resistance', *Sociological Forum*, 19(4): 533–54.

Holmes, O. (2012) 'Anonymous declares internet war on Syria', *ABC News*, 30 November. Available from: https://www.nbcnews.com/tech/tech-news/anonymous-declares-internet-war-syria-flna1c7350148

Holt, T., Freilich, J. and Chermak, S. (2017) 'Exploring the subculture of ideologically motivated cyber-attackers', *Journal of Contemporary Criminal Justice*, 33(3): 212–33.

Horsey, H. R. (1994) 'The duty of care component of the Delaware business judgment rule', *Delaware Journal of Corporate Law*, 19(3): 971–98.

Huazhong, W. (2010) 'Drunken driver boasts father is a police official', *China Daily*, 7 November. Available from: http://www.chinadaily.com.cn/china/2010-10/20/content_11431705.htm

Hunn, D. (2014) 'How Anonymous hackers changed Ferguson, Mo., protests', *Government Technology*, 13 August. Available from: https://www.govtech.com/public-safety/how-computer-hackers-changed-the-ferguson-protests.html

Hunt, G. (1995) *Whistleblowing in the Health Service: Accountability, Law and Professional Practice*, London: Edward Arnold.

Information Warfare Monitor (2009) 'Tracking Ghostnet: investigating a cyber espionage network', 29 March. Available from: http://www.nartv.org/mirror/ghostnet.pdf

Innes, J. (1996) *Privacy, Intimacy and Isolation*, Oxford: Oxford University Press.

Jackson, W. (2011) 'BART website breach exposes divisions within hacktivist group', *GCN*, 18 August. Available from: https://gcn.com/cybersecurity/2011/08/bart-website-breach-exposes-divisions-within-hacktivist-group/282337/

Jackson, R. and Pisoiu, D. (2018) *Contemporary Debates on Terrorism*, Abingdon: Routledge.

Jackson, R., Jarvis, L., Gunning, J. and Breen-Smyth, M. (2011) *Terrorism: A Critical Introduction*, Basingstoke: Palgrave Macmillan.

Jensen, J. V. (1987) 'Ethical tension points in whistleblowing', *Journal of Business Ethics*, 9: 321–8.

Jeter, L. (2003) *Disconnected: Deceit and Betrayal at WorldCom*, Hoboken, NJ: John Wiley and Sons.

Johnson, R. A. (2003) *Whistleblowing: When It Works and Why*, Boulder, CO: Lynne Rienner Publishers.

Johnston, L. (1996) 'What is vigilantism?', *British Journal of Criminology*, 36(2): 220–36.

Jordan, T. (2014) *Internet, Society and Culture Communicative Practices Before and After the Internet*, London: Bloomsbury.

Jordan, T. and Taylor, P. A. (2004) *Hackers and Cyberwars: Rebels with a Cause?*, London: Routledge.

Jos, P. H., Tompkins, M. E. and Hays, S. W. (1989) 'In praise of difficult people: a portrait of the committed whistleblower', *Public Administration Review*, 49(6): 552–61.

Kang, J. (1998) 'Information privacy in cyberspace transactions', *Stanford Law Review*, 50(4): 1193–294.

Kasachkoff, T. (1998) 'Killing in self-defense: an unquestionable or problematic defense?', *Law and Philosophy*, 17(5–6): 509–31.

Keefe, P. (2005) *Chatter: Dispatches from the Secret World of Global Eavesdropping*, New York: Random House.

Kennedy, R. (1997) *Race Crime and the Law*, New York: Pantheon.

King, J. (1998) 'Information in cyberspace transactions', *Stanford Law Review*, 50(4): 1193–294.

Kizza, J. M. (2020) *Guide to Computer Network Security*, Berlin: Springer.

Klein, A. G. (2015) 'Vigilante media: unveiling Anonymous and the hacktivist persona in the global press', *Communication Monographs*, 82(3): 379–401.

Kleinig, J. (1976) 'Good Samaritanism', *Philosophy and Public Affairs*, 5(4): 382–407.

Kono, D. (2006) 'Optimal obfuscation: democracy and trade policy transparency', *American Political Science Review*, 100: 369–84.

Konvitz, M. R. (1966) 'Privacy and the law: a philosophical prelude', *Law and Contemporary Problems*, 31(2): 272–80.

Krauth, A. (2012), 'Anonymous in portmanteaupia', *Social Alternatives*, 31(2): 27–32.

Krebs on Security (2011) 'HBGary Federal hacked by Anonymous', *Krebs on Security*, 7 February. Available from: https://krebsonsecurity.com/2011/02/hbgary-federal-hacked-by-anonymous/

Kumar, M. (2011) 'Anonymous open letter to citizens of United States of America!', *The Hacker News*, 24 March. Available from: https://thehackernews.com/2011/03/anonymous-open-letter-to-citizens-of.html

Kutz, C. (2007) 'Causeless complicity', *Criminal Law and Philosophy*, 1(2): 289–305.

Lackey, D. P. (1989) *The Ethics of War and Peace*, London: Prentice Hall International.

Lam, O. (2010) 'China: my father is Li Gang!' *Global Voices*, 22 October. Available from: https://globalvoices.org/2010/10/22/china-my-father-is-li-gang/

Landler, M. and Markoff, J. (2007) 'In Estonia, what may be the first war in cyberspace', *The New York Times*, 28 May. Available from: https://www.nytimes.com/2007/05/28/business/worldbusiness/28iht-cyberwar.4.5901141.html

Laufer, R. and Wolfe, M. (1977) 'Privacy as a concept and social issue', *The Journal of Social Issues*, 33(3): 22–42.

Laugerud, S. (2021) 'Narrating the harm of rape: how rape victims invoke different models of psychological trauma', *BioSocieties*, 16: 22–40.

Lee, H. (2018) 'A new societal self-defense theory of punishment: the rights-protection theory', *Philosophia*, 46: 337–53.

Lefkowitz, D. (2007) 'On a moral right to civil disobedience', *Ethics*, 117(2): 202–33.

Leigh, D. and Harding, L. (2011) *WikiLeaks: Inside Julian Assange's War on Secrecy*, London: Guardian Books.

Lenard, N. (2012) 'Anonymous takes on Syrian government', *The Salon*, 30 November. Available from: https://www.salon.com/2012/11/30/anonymous_takes_on_syrian_government/

Lennerfors, T. (2007) 'The transformation of transparency: on the act on public procurement and the right to appeal in the context of the war on corruption', *Journal of Business Ethics*, 73(4): 381–90.

Lepora, C. and Goodin, R. (2013) *On Complicity and Compromise*, Oxford: Oxford University Press.

Lever, A. (2005) 'Why racial profiling is hard to justify: a response to Risse and Zeckhauser', *Philosophy and Public Affairs*, 33(1): 94–110.

Leverick, F. (2006) *Killing in Self-Defence*, Oxford: Oxford University Press.

Levy, S. (1984) *Hackers: Heroes of the Computer Revolution*, New York: Doubleday.

Lewis, D. (1989) 'Mill and Milquetoast', *Australasian Journal of Philosophy*, 67: 152–71.

Lewis, J. (2002) 'Assessing the rise of cyber terrorism, cyber war and other cyber threats', Centre for Strategic and International Studies. Available from: https://csis-website-prod.s3.amazonaws.com/s3fs-public/legacy_fi les/files/media/csis/pubs/021101_risks_of_cyberterror.pdf

Li, X. (2013) 'Hacktivism and the First Amendment: drawing the line between cyber protests and crime', *Harvard Journal of Law & Technology*, 7(1): 301–30.

Lindley, R. (1986) *Autonomy*, Basingstoke: Palgrave Macmillan.

List, C. and Goodin, R. E. (2001) 'Epistemic democracy: generalizing the Condorcet jury theorem', *Journal of Political Philosophy*, 9: 277–306.

List, C., Elsholtz, C. and Seeley T. D. (2009) 'Independence and interdependence in collective decision making: an agent-based model of nest-site choice by honeybee swarms', *Philosophical Transactions of the Royal Society B*, 364: 755–62.

Littauer, D. (2013) 'Anonymous hacks Nigeria's government website over anti-gay bill', *LGBTQ Nation*, 5 July. Available from: http://www.lgbt qnation.com/2013/07/anonymous-hacks-nigerias-government-webs ite-over-anti-gay-bill/

Little, C. B. and Sheffield, C. P. (1983) 'Frontiers and criminal justice: English private prosecution societies and American vigilantism in the eighteenth and nineteenth centuries', *American Sociological Review*, 48(6): 796–808.

Liu, A. (2004) *The Laws of Cool: Knowledge Work and the Culture of Information*, Chicago, IL: University of Chicago Press.

Locke, J. (1988)[1689] *Two Treatises of Government*, Cambridge: Cambridge University Press.

Lopez, K. J. (2010) 'On this Sunday outrage', *National Review*, 29 November. Available from: https://www.nationalreview.com/corner/sunday-outr age-kathryn-jean-lopez/

Loveluck, B. (2020) 'The many shades of digital vigilantism: a typology of online self-justice', *Global Crime*, 21(3–4): 213–41.

Lowes, D. E. (2006) *The Anti-Capitalist Dictionary: Movements, Histories and Motivations*, Halifax, Canada: Fernwood Publishing Ltd.

Lu, D. (2015) 'When ethical hackers can't compete', *The Atlantic*, 8 December. Available from: https://www.theatlantic.com/technology/arch ive/2015/12/white-hat-ethical-hacking-cybersecurity/419355/

Luban, D. (2005) 'Liberalism, torture and the ticking bomb', *Virginia Law Review*, 9(6): 1425–61.

Ludlow, P. (2013) 'Aaron Swartz was right', *The Chronical of Higher Education*, 25 February. Available from: https://www.chronicle.com/article/Aaron-Swartz-Was-Right/137425

Lynch, W. and Kline, R. (2000) 'Engineering practice and engineering ethics', *Science, Technology, & Human Values*, 25(2): 195–225.

Lyon, D. (1994) *The Electronic Eye: The Rise of Surveillance Society*, Cambridge: Polity Press.

Mack, E. (1980) 'Bad Samaritanism and causation of harm', *Philosophy and Public Affairs*, 9(3): 230–59.

Mahat, R. (2008) 'A carrot for the lawyer: providing economic incentives for in-house lawyers in a Sarbanes-Oxley Regime', *The Georgetown Journal of Legal Ethics*, 21(3): 913–34.

Manion, M. and Goodrum, A. (2000) 'Terrorism or civil disobedience: towards a hacktivist ethic', *Computers and Society*, 30(2): 14–19.

Mansfield-Devine, S. (2011a) 'Hacktivism: assessing the damage', *Network Security*, 8: 5–13.

Mansfield-Devine, S. (2011b) 'Anonymous: serious threat or mere annoyance?', *Network Security*, 11(1): 4–10.

Markel, D. (2011) 'What might retributive justice be? An argument for the confrontational conception of retributivism', in M. White (ed), *Retributivism. Essays on Theory and Policy*, Oxford: Oxford University Press, pp 49–72.

Martin, R. (1970) 'Civil disobedience', *Ethics*, 80(1): 123–39.

Marx, G. (1998) 'Ethics for the new surveillance', *The Information Society*, 14(3): 171–85.

Marx, G. (2004) 'Some concepts that may be useful in understanding the myriad forms and contexts of surveillance', *Intelligence and National Security*, 19(2): 234.

Mazzetti, M. (2015) 'CIA report found value of brutal interrogation was inflated', *The New York Times*, 20 January. Available from: http://www.nytimes.com/2015/01/21/world/cia-report-found-value-of-brutal-interr ogation-was-inflated.html?_r=1

McAdam, D. (1982) *Political Process and the Development of Black Insurgency*, Chicago, IL: University of Chicago Press.

McAfee and the Center for Strategic and International Studies (2013) *The Economic Impact of Cybercrime and Cyber Espionage*, July. Available from: http://csis.org/files/publication/60396rpt_cybercrime-cost_071 3_ph4_0.pdf

McArthur, R. (2001) 'Reasonable expectations of privacy', *Ethics and Information Technology*, 3: 123–8.

McCahill, M. (1998) 'Beyond Foucault: towards a contemporary theory of surveillance', in C. Norris, J. Moran, and G. Armstrong (eds), *Surveillance, Closed-Circuit Television and Social Control*, Aldershot: Ashgate, pp 41–65.

McCormick, T. (2013) 'Anthropology of an idea: hacktivism', *Foreign Policy*, 200: 24–5.

McGlynn, J. and Richardson, B. K. (2014) 'Private support, public alienation: whistle-blowers and the paradox of social support', *Western Journal of Communication*, 78(2): 213–37.

McGoogan, C., Titcomb, J. and Krol, C. (2017) 'What is WannaCry and how does ransomware work?', *The Telegraph*, 18 May. Available from: http://www.telegraph.co.uk/technology/0/ransomware-does-work/

McMahan, J. (1994) 'Innocence, self-defence and killing in war', *The Journal of Political Philosophy*, 2(1): 193–221.

McMahan, J. (2006) 'On the moral equality of combatants', *Journal of Political Philosophy*, 14(4): 377–93.

McPherson, R., Houmansadr, A. and Shmatikov, V. (2016) 'Covertcast: using live streaming to evade internet censorship', *Proceedings on Privacy Enhancing Technologies*, 3: 212–25.

McReynolds, P. (2015) 'How to think about cyber conflict involving non-state actors', *Philosophy and Technology*, 28: 427–48.

Menn, J. (2019) *Cult of the Dead Cow: How the Original Hacking Supergroup Might Just Save the World*, New York: Public Affairs.

Merton, R. (1968) *Social Theory and Social Structure*, New York: Free Press.

metac0m (2003) 'What is hacktivism 2.0', *The Hacktivist*, December. Available from: http://edshare.soton.ac.uk/8762/2/whatishacktivism.pdf

Metz, C. (2008) 'Anonymous hacks Sarah Palin's Yahoo! Account', *The Register*, 17 September. Available from: http://www.theregister.co.uk/2008/09/17/anonymous_hacks_sarah_palin/

Meyers, D. T. (1995) 'Rights in collision: a non-punitive compensatory remedy for abusive speech', *Law and Philosophy*, 14: 203–43.

Mill, J. S. (1968) *On Liberty*, in M. Cowling (ed.) *Selected Writings of John Stuart Mill*, New York: The New American Library, p 121.

Mill, J. S. (1991) *On Liberty*, ed. John Gray, Oxford: Oxford University Press.

Mill, J. S. (2005) *On Liberty*, New York: Cosimo.

Miller, A. (1971) *The Assault on Privacy: Computers, Databanks and Dossiers*, Michigan: University of Michigan Press.

Milone, M. G. (2002) 'Hacktivism: securing the national infrastructure', *The Business Lawyer*, 58(1): 383–413.

Milton, J. (1968 [1644]) *Areopagitica*, New York: New York University Press.

Modighaini, A. and Rachel, F. (1995) 'The role of interaction sequences and the timing of resistance in shaping obedience and defiance to authority', *Journal of Social Issues*, 51: 107–23.

Monagham, H. P. (1977) 'Of liberty and property', *Cornell Law Review*, 62(1): 404–44.

Monroe, A. and Malle, B. (2014) 'Free will without metaphysics', in A. R. Mele (ed.), *Surrounding Free Will*, New York: Oxford University Press, pp 25–48.

Montague, P. (1989) 'The morality of self-defense: a reply of Wasserman', *Philosophy and Public Affairs*, 18(1): 81–9.

Moore, A. (2011) 'Privacy, security, and government surveillance: Wikileaks and the new accountability', *Public Affairs Quarterly*, 25(2): 141–56.

Moore, M. (2010) *Placing Blame: A Theory of Criminal Law*, Oxford: Oxford University Press.

Morris, A. (1984) *The Origins of the Civil Rights Movement*, New York: Free Press.

Morris, K. (2013) 'Anonymous has finally released the names of Rehtaeh Parsons's alleged rapists', *Daily Dot*, 24 July. Available from: http://www.dailydot.com/news/rehtaeh-parsons-rapists-names-identity-revealed-anonymous/

Morrissey, D. (1997) *Disclosure and Secrecy: Security Classification Executive Orders*, Columbia: AEJMC.

Murphy, J. G. (2007) 'Legal moralism and retribution revisited', *Criminal Law and Philosophy*, 1: 5–20.

Murphy, S. (2011) 'Agents provocateurs: hacktivists have noisily exposed the sorry state of internet security', *New Scientist*, 10 September.

Musil, S. (2012) 'Anonymous declares war on Syrian government', *CNet*, 29 November. Available from: https://www.cnet.com/tech/services-and-software/anonymous-declares-war-on-syrian-government-web-sites/

Nagel, T. (1986) *The View from Nowhere*, Oxford: Oxford University Press.

Nagel, T. (1995) 'Personal rights and public space', *Philosophy and Public Affairs*, 24: 83–107.

Naughton, J. (2000) *A Brief History of the Future: Origins of the Internet*, London: Phoenix.

Near, J. and Miceli, M. (1995) 'Effective whistleblowing', *Academy of Management Review*, 20(3): 679–708.

The New York Times (2010) 'A note to readers: the decision to punish diplomatic documents', 28 November. Available from: https://www.nytimes.com/2010/11/29/world/29editornote.html

Nobles, R. and Schiff, D. (2002) 'The right to appeal and workable systems of justice', *The Modern Law Review*, 65(5): 676–701.

Norman, R. (1995) *Ethics, Killing and War*, Cambridge: Cambridge University Press.

Norton, Q. (2012) 'How Anonymous picks targets, launches attacks, and takes powerful organizations down', *Wired*, 3 July. Available from: https://www.wired.com/2012/07/ff-anonymous/

Nozick, R. (1974) *Anarchy, State, and Utopia*, New York: Basic Books.

Nussbaum, M. (2000) *Women and Human Development: The Capabilities Approach*, Cambridge: Cambridge University Press.

Ochi, M. (2016) 'Gravity threshold before the International Criminal Court: an overview of the court's practice', *International Crimes Database Brief*, 19 January: 1–16.

Olson, P. (2011) 'Anonymous hacks BART after cellphone blockade', *Forbes*, 15 August. Available from: https://www.forbes.com/sites/parmyolson/2011/08/15/anonymous-hacks-bart-after-cellphone-blockade/

O'Malley, G. (2013) 'Hacktivism: cyber-activism or cyber-crime', *Trinity College Law Review*, 16: 137–60.

O'Neil, L. (2015) 'Anonymous plans to "unhood" 1,000 Ku Klux Klan members online', CBC News, 29 October. Available from: https://www.cbc.ca/news/trending/anonymous-plans-to-reveal-the-identities-of-1-000-kkk-members-1.3295523

Ong, G. (2016) 'IT grad, 23, arrested for Comelec website hack', *The Philippine Star*, 22 April. Available from: http://www.philstar.com/headlines/2016/04/22/1575594/it-grad-23-arrested-comelec-website-hack

Orend, B. (2006) *The Morality of War*, Calgary: Broadview Press.

Otsuka, M. (1994) 'Killing the innocent in self-defense', *Philosophy and Public Affairs*, 23(1): 74–94.

Owen, T. (2015) *Disruptive Power: The Crisis of the State in the Digital Age*, Oxford: Oxford University Press.

Padmanabhan, S. (2012) 'Hacking for Lulz1: employing expert hackers to combat cyber terrorism', *Vanderbilt Journal of Entertainment and Technology Law*, 15(1): 191–226.

Paine, S. (2000) *Endangered Spaces: Privacy, Law and the Home*, CAMC Publications.

Pattison, J. (2018) *The Alternatives to War: From Sanctions to Nonviolence*, Oxford: Oxford University Press.

Pedhazur, A. and Perliger, A. (2003) 'The causes of vigilant political violence: the case of Jewish settlers', *Civil Wars*, 6(3): 9–30.

Perlroth, N. (2014) 'Anonymous hackers' efforts to identify Ferguson police officer create turmoil', *The New York Times*, 14 August. Available from: https://www.nytimes.com/2014/08/15/us/ferguson-case-roils-collective-called-anonymous.html

Pfaff, T. and Tiel, J. (2004) 'The ethics of espionage', *The Journal of Military Ethics*, 3(1): 1–15.

Phillips, R. (1984) *War and Justice*, Norman: University of Oklahoma Press.

Poeter, D. (2011) 'Anonymous BART protest shuts down several underground stations', *PCMag*, 16 August. Available from: https://uk.pcmag.com/news/111848/anonymous-bart-protest-shuts-down-seve ral-underground-stations

Pogge, T. (1991) 'Coercion and violence', in J. Brady and N. Garver (eds), *Justice, Law and Violence*, Philadelphia, PA: Temple University Press, pp 65–9.

Polyviou, P. (1982) *Search and Seizure: Constitutional and Common Law*, London: Duckworth.

Posner, G. (2017) 'China's secret cyberterrorism' (updated), *The Daily Beast*, 14 July. Available from: http://www.thedailybeast.com/articles/2010/01/13/chinas-secret-cyber-terrorism.html

Post, R. (1991) 'Racist speech, democracy, and the First Amendment', *William and Mary Law Review*, 32: 267–327.

Post, R. (1993) 'Managing deliberation: the quandary of democratic dialogue', *Ethics*, 103: 654–78.

Pozen, D. (2016) 'Privacy-privacy tradeoffs', *The University of Chicago Law Review*, 83(1): 221–47.

Prasdas, A. and Prasad, P. (1998) 'Everyday struggles at the workplace: the nature and implications of routine resistance in contemporary organizations', *Research in the Sociology of Organizations*, 15: 225–57.

Profitt, N. J. (1996) '"Battered women" as "victims" and "survivors": creating space for resistance', *Canadian Social Work Review/Revue Canadienne de Service Social*, 13(1): 23–38.

Purshouse, J. (2019) 'Paedophile hunters: how citizen-led policing is putting people's lives at risk', *The Conversation*, 22 January. Available at: https://theconversation.com/paedophile-hunters-how-citizenled-policing-is-putt ing-peoples-lives-at-risk-110006

Raggi, R. (1977) 'An independent right to freedom of association', *Harvard Civil Rights-Civil Liberties Law Review*, 12(1): 1–30.

Rangarajan, L. N. (1998) 'Diplomacy, states and secrecy in communications', *Diplomacy & Statecraft*, 9(3): 18–24.

Rawls, J. (1971) *Theory of Justice*, Cambridge, MA: Harvard University Press.

Rawls, J. (1977) *Theory of Justice*, Cambridge: Cambridge University Press.

Rawls, J. (2007) *Lectures on the History of Political Philosophy*, ed. Samuel Freeman, Cambridge, MA: Harvard University Press.

Rawls, J. (2009) 'The justification of civil disobedience', in A. Kavanagh and J. Oberdiek (eds), *Arguing about Law*, Abingdon: Routledge, pp 244–53.

Raz, J. (1986) *The Morality of Freedom*, Oxford: Clarendon Press.

Razmetaeva, Y. (2014) 'The right to resist and the right to rebellion', *Jurisprudence*, 21(3): 758–84.

Reed, M. G., Syverson, P. and Goldschlag, D. (1998) 'Anonymous connections and onion routing', *IEEE Journal on Selected Areas in Communications*, 16(4): 482–94.

Reiman, J. H. (1976) 'Privacy, intimacy, and personhood', *Philosophy and Public Affairs*, 5(1): 26–44.

Rescher, N. (1972) *Welfare: The Social Issue in Philosophical Perspective*, Pittsburgh, PA: University of Pittsburgh Press.

Reynolds, P. (2015) 'How to think about cyber conflicts involving non-state actors', *Philosophy and Technology*, 28(3): 427–48.

Richmond, S. (2011) 'Millions of internet users hit by massive Sony PlayStation data theft', *The Telegraph*, 26 April. Available from: https://www.telegraph.co.uk/technology/sony/8475728/Millions-of-internet-users-hit-by-massive-Sony-PlayStation-data-theft.html

Robinson, M. (2000) 'The construction and reinforcement of the myth of race crime', *Journal of Contemporary Criminal Justice*, 16: 133–56.

Robinson, T. (1995) 'Gentrification and grassroots resistance in San Francisco's Tenderloin', *Urban Affairs Review*, 30: 382–513.

Rogers, A. (2014) 'What Anonymous is doing in Ferguson', *Time*, 21 August. Available from: http://time.com/3148925/ferguson-michael-brown-anonymous/

Rosenbaum, H. J. and Sederberg, P. C. (1974) 'Vigilantism: an analysis of establishment violence', *Comparative Politics*, 6(4): 541–70.

Rosenbaum, T. (2004) *The Myth of Moral Justice*, London: HarperCollins.

Rothschild, J. and Miethe, T. (1999) 'Whistle-blower disclosures and management retaliation', *Work and Occupations*, 26(1): 107–28.

RT.Com (2014) '#TangoDown: Anonymous close Cleveland City govt website over 12yo shooting death', *RT.com*, 24 November. Available from: https://www.rt.com/usa/208255-anonymous-cleveland-police-shooting/

Ruffin, O. (2001) 'The hacktivismo declaration', *Cult of the Dead Cow*, 4 July. Available from: https://www.digitalmanifesto.net/manifestos/197/

Sachan, A. (2012) 'Countering terrorism through dark web analysis', *Computing Communication & Networking Technologies,* Third International Conference.

Sagar, R. (2016) *Secrets and Leaks: The Dilemma of State Secrecy,* Princeton, NJ: Princeton University Press.

Sanger, D. (2012) 'Obama order sped up wave of cyberattacks against Iran', *The New York Times*, 1 June. Available from: http://www.nytimes.com/2012/06/01/world/middleeast/obama-ordered-wave-of-cyberattacks-against-iran.html

Sankowski, E. (1992) 'Blame and autonomy', *American Philosophical Quarterly*, 29(3): 291–9.

Sauter, M. (2015) *The Coming Swarm: DDoS Actions, Hacktivism, and Civil Disobedience on the Internet*, New York: Bloomsbury.

Scanlon, T. (1972) 'A theory of freedom of expression', *Philosophy and Public Affairs*, 1: 204–26.

Scanlon, T. (1979) 'Freedom of expression and categories of expression', *University of Pittsburgh Law Review*, 40: 519–50.

Scanlon, T. M. and Daney, J. (2000) 'Intention and permissibility', *Supplement to the Proceedings of the Aristotelian Society*, 74(1): 301–17.

Schauer, F. (1993) 'The phenomenology of speech and harm', *Ethics*, 103: 635–53.

Scheuerman, W. (2016) 'Digital disobedience in the law', *New Political Science*, 38(3): 299–314.

Schneier, B. (2006) *Beyond Fear: Thinking Sensibly about Security in an Uncertain World*, Berlin: Springer.

Schwartz, B. (1961) 'The Supreme Court: October 1959 term', *Michigan Law Review*, 593: 403–30.

Scott, J. (1985) *Weapons of the Weak: Everyday Forms of Peasant Resistance*, New Haven, CT: Yale University Press.

Serracino-Inglott, P. (2013) 'Is it OK to be an Anonymous?', *Ethics & Global Politics*, 6(1): 217–44.

Shapiro, I. (2003) *The Moral Foundations of Politics*, New Haven, CT: Yale University Press.

Sheoran, P. and Singh, S. (2014) 'Applications of ethical hackers', *International Journal of Enhanced Research in Science Technology & Engineering*, 3(5): 112–14.

Shils, E. (1966) 'Privacy: its constitution and vicissitudes', *Law and Contemporary Problems*, 31(2): 281–306.

Shirky, C. (2008) *Here Comes Everybody*, New York: Penguin Press.

Shotland, R. L. (1976) 'Spontaneous vigilantes', *Society*, 13(3): 30–2.

Silberstein, S. (2004) *War of Worlds: Language, Politics and 9/11*, London: Routledge.

Simitis, S. (1987) 'Reviewing privacy in an information age', *University of Pennsylvania Law Review*, 35(3): 707–46.

Singer, P. (1972) 'Famine, affluence, and morality', *Philosophy and Public Affairs*, 7(2): 229–43.

Singer, P. (2003) *Corporate Warriors: The Rise of the Privatized Military Industry*, Ithaca: Cornell University Press.

Slim, H. (2002) *Killing Civilians: Methods, Madness and Morality in War*, Basingstoke: Palgrave.

Smallridge, J., Wagner, P. and Crowl, J. (2016) 'Understanding cyber-vigilantism: a conceptual framework', *Journal of Theoretical and Philosophical Criminology*, 8(1): 57–70.

Smith, A. (1976) *The Theory of Moral Sentiments*, Oxford: Clarendon Press.

Smith, M. B. E. (1973) 'Is there a prima facie obligation to obey the law?', *The Yale Law Review*, 82(5): 950–76.

Smith, P. (1990) 'The duty to rescue and the slippery slope problem', *Social Theory and Practice*, 16(1): 19–41.

Solove, D. (2004) *The Digital Person: Technology and Privacy in the Information Age*, New York: New York University Press.

Solove, D. (2007a) 'I've got nothing to hide and other misunderstandings of privacy', *San Diageo Law Review*, 44: 745–72.

Solove, D. (2007b) *The Future of Reputation: Gossip, Rumor, and Privacy on the Internet*, London: Yale University Press.

Sommer, P. and Brown, I. (2011) 'Reducing systemic cybersecurity risk', *Organisation for Economic Cooperation and Development*, 14 January. Available from: http://ssrn.com/abstract=1743384

Staff, R. (2014) 'JPMorgan hack exposed data of 83 million, among biggest breaches in history', *Reuters*, 3 October. Available from: https://www.reuters.com/article/us-jpmorgan-cybersecurity-idUSKCN0HR23T20141003

Steger, M. (2003) *Judging Nonviolence: The Dispute between Realists and Idealists*, London: Routledge.

Stephey, M. J. (2008) 'Sarah Palin's email hacked', *Time*, 17 September. Available from: http://content.time.com/time/politics/article/0,8599,1842097,00.html

Sterling, T. (2002) *The Enron Scandal*, New York: Nova Science Publishing.

Stiglitz, J. (1999) 'On liberty, the right to know, and public discourse: the role of transparency in public life', in M. J. Gibny (ed.), *Globalising Rights: Oxford Amnesty Lecture 1999*, pp 1–32.

Stone, J. (2014) 'Tamir rice shooting inspires anonymous hack on Cleveland websites', *International Business Times*, 24 November. Available from: http://www.ibtimes.com/tamir-rice-shooting-inspires-anonymous-hack-cleveland-websites-1728681

Stone, M. (2011) 'Operation BART: Anonymous protests San Fran cell phone censorship', *Examiner.com*, 14 August. Available from: http://www.examiner.com/anonymous-in-national/operation-bart-anonymous-protests-san-fran-cell-phone-censorship

Strauss, D. (1991) 'Persuasion, autonomy, and freedom of expression', *Columbia Law* Review, 91: 334–1.

Strossen, N. (1990) 'Regulating racist speech on campus: a modest proposal?', *Duke Law Journal*, 1990: 484–572.

Sunstein, C. (2005) *Laws of Fear: Beyond the Precautionary Principle*, Cambridge: Cambridge University Press.

Tan, L. (2016) 'Website claims: registered voters' sensitive data easily searchable', *CNN Philippines*, 21 April. *Available from:* http://cnnphilippines.com/news/2016/04/21/Comelec-hack-data-registered-Filipino-voters.html

Tanczer, L. (2017) 'The terrorist – hacker/hacktivist distinction: an investigation of self-identified hackers and hacktivists', in M. Conway, L. Jarvis, O. Lehane, S. Macdonald and L. Nouri (eds), *Terrorists' Use of the Internet*, Amsterdam: IOS Press, pp 77–92.

Taylor, P. and Harris, J. (2006) 'Hacktivism', in H. Bidgoli (ed.), *Handbook of Information Security: Information Warfare; Social Issues, Legal and International Issues; and Security Foundations, Vol.2*, Hoboken, NJ: Wiley, pp 172–82.

Thomas, D. (2002) *Hacker Culture*, Minneapolis: University of Minnesota Press.

Thompson, D. F. (1999) 'Democratic secrecy', *Political Science Quarterly*, 114(2): 181–93.

Thompson, P. B. (2001) 'Privacy, secrecy and security', *Ethics and Information Technology*, 3: 13–19.

Thomson, J. J. (1975) 'The right to privacy', *Philosophy and Public Affairs*, 4(4): 295–314.

Thomson, J. J. (1986) *Rights, Restitution and Risk: Essays in Moral Theory*, Cambridge, MA: Harvard University Press.

Thomson, J. J. (1991) 'Self-defence', *Philosophy and Public Affairs*, 20(4): 283–310.

Thorsen, E., Sreedharan, C. and Allan, S. (2013) 'WikiLeaks and whistle-blowing: the framing of Bradley Manning', in B. Brevini, A. Hintz and P. McCurdy (eds), *Beyond Wikileaks: Implications for the Future of Communications, Journalism and Society*, Basingstoke: Palgrave Macmillan, pp 101–22.

Tidy, J. (2022) 'Anonymous: how hackers are trying to undermine Putin', BBC News, 20 March. Available from https://www.bbc.co.uk/news/technology-60784526

TOR (nd) 'What protections does TOR provide?'. Available from: https://www.torproject.org/docs/faq.html.en#WhatProtectionsDoesTorProvide

TOR (2015) 'Learning more about the GFW's active probing system', *The TOR Project*, 14 September. Available from: https://blog.torproject.org/category/tags/china

Traynor, I. (2007) 'Russia accused of unleashing cyberwar to disable Estonia', *The Guardian*, 17 May. Available from: http://www.guardian.co.uk/world/2007/may/17/topstories3.russia

Trottier, D. (2017) 'Digital vigilantism as weaponisation of visibility', *Philosophy and Technology*, 30: 55–72.

Tuma, S. E. (2011) 'What does CFAA mean and why should I care: a primer on the Computer Fraud and Abuse Act for civil litigators', *South Carolina Law Review*, 63(1): 142–90.

UNESCO (2015) *Keystones to Foster Inclusive Knowledge Societies: Access to Information and Knowledge, Freedom of Expression, Privacy, and Ethics on a Global Internet*, Paris: UNESCO Publishing. Available from: http://unesdoc.unesco.org/images/0023/002325/232563e.pdf

US Senate Select Committee (2014) *Committee Study of the Central Intelligence Agency's Detention and Interrogation Program*. Available from: http://fas.org/irp/congress/2014_rpt/ssci-rdi.pdf

Utterback, J. (2013) 'Cases of hacktivism', *Hacktivism 101*, 28 May. Available from: https://joymargret89.wordpress.com/2013/05/28/cases-of-hacktivism/

Vamosi, R. (2008) 'Anonymous hackers take on the Church of Scientology', *CNET*, 25 January. Available from: https://www.cnet.com/news/anonymous-hackers-take-on-the-church-of-scientology/

Wagenseil, P. (2011) 'Anonymous "hacktivists" attack Egyptian websites', *Security News Daily*, 6 January. Available from: http://www.msnbc.msn.com/id/41280813/ns/technology_and_science-security/#.T3bs0r9SR7E

Waldron, J. (2003) 'Security and liberty: the image of balance', *Journal of Political Philosophy*, 11(2): 191–210.

Walzer, M. (2000) *Just and Unjust Wars: A Moral Argument with Historical Arguments*, New York: Basic Books.

Wang, F., Zeng, D., Hendler, J. A., Zhang, Q., Feng, Z., Gao, Y. et al (2010) 'A study of the Human Flesh search engine: crowd-powered expansion of online knowledge', *Computer*, 43(8): 45–53.

Waqas (2014) 'Anonymous shuts down city of Cleveland website', *HackRead*, 26 November. Available from: https://www.hackread.com/anonymous-shuts-city-cleveland-website/

Wasserman, D. (1987) 'Justifying self-defense', *Philosophy and Public Affairs*, 164(4): 356–78.

Weaver, W. and Pallitto, R. (2005) 'State secrets and executive powers', *Political Science Quarterly*, 120(1): 85–112.

Webb, M. (2021) *Coding Democracy: How Hackers Are Disrupting Power, Surveillance Authoritarianism*, Cambridge, MA: MIT Press.

Weinstein, M. A. (1971) 'The uses of privacy in the good life', in J. R. Pennock and J. W. Chapman (eds), *Privacy: Nomos XIII*, New York: Atherton Press, pp 88–104.

Wells, C. (2004) 'National security and the Freedom of Information Act', *Administrative Law Review*, 56(4): 1195–222.

Westin, A. (1967) *Privacy and Freedom*, London: Bodley Head.

Whelan, J. M. (1991) 'Charity and the duty to rescue', *Social Theory and Practice*, 17(3): 441–56.

Wiemann, G. (2004) 'Cyberterrorism: how real is the threat?' *United States Institute for Peace*, 119: 2–12.

Williams, G. (2003) 'Blame and responsibility', *Ethical Thought and Moral Practice*, 6: 427–45.

Williams, J. (2008) 'Space, scale and just war: meeting the challenge of humanitarian intervention and trans-national terrorism', *Review of International Studies*, 34(4): 581–600.

Wilmot, S. (2000) 'Nurses and whistleblowing: the ethical issues', *Philosophical and Ethical Issues*, 32(5): 1051–7.

Wong, J. C. (2016) 'Activists lose criminal case on climate change defense – but judge praises effort', *The Guardian*, 15 January. Available from: https://www.theguardian.com/environment/2016/jan/15/delta-5-seattle-washington-climate-change-court-defense

Woodcock, B. (2011) 'Overview of the Egyptian internet shutdown', *Packet Clearing House*, February. Available from: https://privacywonk.net/download/Egypt-PCH-Overview.pdf

Wray, S. (1999) 'On electronic civil disobedience', *Peace Review*, 11(1): 107–11.

Xu, B. and Shaoting, J. (2008) 'Human flesh engine: an internet lynching?', *Xinhua News*, July 4. Available from: http://news.xinhuanet.com/english/2008-07/04/content_8491087.htm

Zedner, L. (2007) 'Pre-crime and post criminology', *Theoretical Criminology*, 11(2): 261–81.

Zelizer, B. and Allan, S. (2010) *Keywords in News and Journalism Studies*, Maidenhead and New York: Open University Press.

Zetter, K. (2008) 'Palin E-mail hacker says it was easy', *Wired*, 18 September. Available from: https://www.wired.com/2008/09/palin-e-mail-ha/

Zimring, F. (2003) *The Contradictions of American Capital Punishment*, Oxford: Oxford University Press.

Index

References to footnotes show both the page number and the note number (5n2).